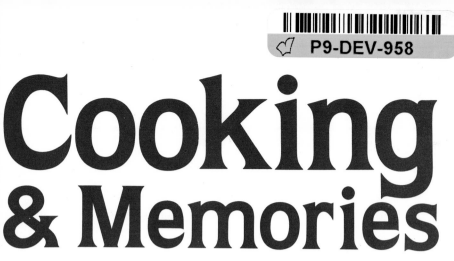

Cooking
& Memories

Favorite Recipes from 20 Mennonite and Amish Cooks

By Phyllis Pellman Good

Photography by Kenneth R. Pellman

a People's Place Booklet

Good Books

Design by Craig Heisey

COOKING AND MEMORIES, Favorite Recipes from 20
Mennonite and Amish Cooks
Copyright © 1983 by Good Books, Lancaster, PA 17602
International Standard Book Number: 0-9346-7216-4
Library of Congress Catalog Card Number: 82-084537

Contents

1 Filling Up on Food and Love

There is no way you can separate food from pleasure when you talk to Betty Pellman—or eat one of her meals! Her love of food and skill as a cook started years ago with her mother as a model. I know because I have been one of the regulars at both these women's tables! Betty is my mother, henceforth known as "Ma" in these pages. Anna S. Neff was my grandmother (Ma refers to her as "Mother."). Together they cultivated a food tradition that was nourishing and succulent—and one that I rely on now that I'm my own family's cook.

Ma grew up with her one sister, Anna, at a busy rural intersection. They lived in an "almost farmhouse" backed up by a small barn and a few acres of land. Her mother's build gave an immediate clue to her own skills at the stove—at four feet eleven inches she weighed 250 pounds.

Ma remembers that her mother was a cookie baker beyond compare. "Mother baked sugar cookies, crumb cakes, and molasses cookies for market. She didn't stand on market herself; she sent the baked things with somebody else. And as a child I was allowed to put the raisins on the tops of the sugar cookies and paint the egg mixture on the molasses cookies. I couldn't stir the batter; it was too stiff and we had no mixer. Mother always dropped the cookies on the baking sheets. She could do it so evenly. All that cookie baking was the way she supplemented our family's income."

Going to market as standholders or preparing food to be sold there were natural practices for many Mennonite and Amish cooks

Betty Pellman likes eating good food. That partly explains her success as a cook. She draws on two other resources—a zest to experiment and the memory of her mother's many satisfying dishes.

Meet my mother—a beloved grandmother, full-time bookkeeper at a nearby college, and a member of a Mennonite congregation in the Lancaster Conference!

and farmers. These people had the bounty to share—either from their truckpatches or ovens—and they didn't need to compromise any principles to do it. Either they operated a market stand as a family, or they prepared the food at home with the help of their children, grandparents, or aunts and uncles. And Grandma fit the tradition! Her younger daughter caught her spirit—and picked up many tempting tricks in the kitchen.

From her mother, Ma learned wonderful ways to make a little bit of good meat stretch to fill a tableful. "Our butcher came to the door a couple times a week. We'd go out into his big refrigerated truck to get the few cuts of meat Mother would buy. One thing she often got was a quarter pound of chipped dried beef. She used that to make creamed dried beef. She would cut toasted bread into little squares and have that on our plates when we came to the table. Then we ladled the creamed beef over top. For our family I would often serve the gravy over steamed or baked potatoes."

Creamed Dried Beef

4 Tbsp. butter or margarine
¼ lb. dried beef, thinly sliced
4 Tbsp. flour
2½ cups milk

Melt butter in skillet. Tear dried beef into shreds and drop into the butter. Stir to coat with butter and then let cook until beef browns around the edges.

Dust beef with flour. Let that mixture brown. Add milk gradually, stirring continuously, while cooking over a low heat.

Cook until gravy has thickened and is smooth.

Makes 4-6 servings

The butcher also brought pig stomachs. Fancy people called the delicacy "hog maw" but the Neffs used the common name. It never colored their enjoyment of the dish. "We usually ate stuffed pig stomach several times each winter," Ma smiles. "Mother and Anna liked the filling; Papa and I preferred the skin. We all liked the ends of the stomachs—they're thicker—so we always cut each in half. And there was always more filling than would fit into the stomach, so we had a casserole with the sausage-potato mixture that baked alongside the stomach.

"Pig stomachs used to be a quarter. Now you have to order them. And they cost two dollars and a quarter!"

Ma's working as a full-time bookkeeper hasn't slackened her zest for family celebrations. Occasionally she whips up a surprise for our birthday meals. But usually she asks what we'd like her to make. There's scarcely been a year when someone hasn't requested stuffed pig stomach. I guess it's the birthday person who lays claim to at least one of the crispy thick and chewy stomach ends. But the rest of us have our eyes on the remaining ends! The years have added politeness to our behavior but time hasn't thinned our enthusiasm for those special pieces of meat!

Pig Stomach

1 large, well cleaned pig stomach
1½ lbs. bulk sausage meat
6 medium potatoes, peeled and diced
1 small onion, chopped

Cook potatoes and onion together until potatoes are tender. Separate sausage meat into small pieces and add to potato mixture. Stir and cook only until sausage loses its reddish color.

Drain off excess liquid. Stuff mixture loosely into stomach and close all openings with skewers laced with string. Place in roast pan with 1/2 cup water. Place remaining mixture that will not fit in stomach in a buttered casserole.

Cover roast pan containing the stomach and bake at 350° for 2-2½ hours. After first hour prick stomach with sharp fork. Place casserole of remaining mixture in oven, uncovered and bake only for the last 40-45 minutes of baking time.

Overstuffing the stomach may cause it to burst while baking because the stomach shrinks considerably.

Makes 4 servings

"We always liked a fat old hen for chicken corn soup," Ma says. "It made such a rich broth. We bought live chickens and dressed our own. I remember Mother boiling hot water, then dipping the chicken and plucking their feathers. She never cut the heads off. That was Papa's job!

"When they were dressed she cut the chickens in pieces, stewed them, cut the meat off the bone, and put it back in the pot with her own canned corn."

Here enters another Pennsylvania Dutch invention—dough balls! "Mother would often add dough balls or rivels to the soup right before serving it. You could make a bunch of them with one egg, so they were an economy measure. And she knew just how to make them. You always wanted to be sure you had some in your bowl!"

Grandma used rivels only in chicken corn soup. Others believe that rivels enhance—and stretch—almost any variety of soup, from potato to rice to pea.

Chicken Corn Soup

3-4 lbs. stewing chicken
salt to taste
water
2 quarts corn, fresh, frozen, or canned
rivels (optional)
3-4 hard-boiled eggs, diced (optional)
dash of pepper

In large kettle cover chicken pieces with water. Salt to taste. Cook until tender, then cut meat off bones and dice into bite-sized pieces.

Return chicken to broth. Add corn and bring to a boil. Stir in rivels or hard-boiled eggs and cook until rivels are cooked through. Add pepper and serve.

Makes 8-10 servings

Rivels
¾ cup flour
1 egg

Put flour in bowl. Break in egg and mix with a fork until dry and crumbly. Drop rivels into boiling soup, stirring to prevent them from packing together.

Sunday noon meal preparation usually happened on Saturday, at least what was practical to do ahead of time. That allowed the cook to concentrate more fully during Sunday morning church. Certain routines developed. "Mother often cooked sweet potatoes on Saturdays. Then we ate them in the skin, spread with butter, on Saturday night. What was left over, she fried for Sunday lunch.

"Usually our main family meal was at suppertime because Papa worked away. But on Sundays we had our big meal at noon. So Sunday evening we ate a lunch—steamed crackers, bologna and cheese, usually pickles and olives, and warm cornstarch!"

Cornstarch is a pudding made from scratch and thickened with cornstarch. Thus, its nickname. Sometimes called "Pap" or "pap soup," the vanilla variety was often made for tiny babies in the days before packaged cereals were made for infants. But *chocolate* cornstarch was the Neff specialty.

Ma remembers, "We ate it warm! We couldn't wait for it to cool."

And cornstarch is still a hit. I prefer mine cold. But we have two daughters who pull up chairs beside their grandma and begin work on a bowlful of the still steaming pudding! Makes me wonder if half the pleasure of food is the company you keep while eating it!

I have certainly been rich in both—the food I've been served and the clan who's shared it with me. Thank you, Ma! Thanks, Grandma.

Chocolate Cornstarch Pudding

3 Tbsp. cornstarch
1/3 cup sugar
1/2 tsp. salt
3 Tbsp. cocoa
2 cups milk
1 tsp. vanilla

Mix dry ingredients well. In a saucepan heat 1½ cups milk. Add other 1/2 cup milk to the dry ingredients and stir until smooth.

When the milk is hot, but before a skin forms, stir in the dampened dry ingredients. Stir constantly over heat until the mixture thickens and comes to a gentle boil (it should not boil vigorously). Remove from heat and serve either warm or cold.

Makes 4-6 servings

2 Cooking with the Seasons

There are few cooks who are more modest than Ruth Good. Nor are there many who are more accomplished.

Ask any of her seven sons what her best dishes are and the list stretches tirelessly, and trails into stories—ham loaf, dinner rolls, cream-filled doughnuts, oyster filling, rhubarb pie, oven fried chicken . . .

There were times when cooking became a burden for her, she once told me quietly, soon after I had become her daughter-in-law. I was exclaiming about my discovery that if I followed recipes to the letter, I got edible food. (Clearly I was the green novice; she was the craftswoman!)

In that moment she opened a window into her world as a farm-wife and mother who regularly cooked three substantial meals for her husband, seven boys-becoming-men, and often, a hired man. In addition to that, she was the family baker, gardener, food preserver, and butcher's helper.

Yet despite all that history, she still shows her affection for her family by presenting us with irresistible food. Years ago we learned that to talk Mother out of filling her table (and, in turn, us) whenever we came home was to deprive her of giving us love.

Mother's cooking days began before tin-canned foods, TV dinners and pie dough sticks. She remembers that their menus reflected the seasons. " 'Ham, mashed potatoes, and dandelion' was a springtime meal when the men were beginning to plow and I was housecleaning. I'd fry ham slices as we got near the end of the

Ruth Good's boys are all gone from home now. But whipping up big meals is something Merle's mother still does regularly. Most often the feasts are for visiting ministers or church families or some of their own kin. Dad is a mostly retired minister in a Lancaster Conference congregation, but he and Mother still do a sizable share of hosting.

winter's supply of home-smoked ham. And I would mash potatoes that were left from the winter. Our gravy came from the ham drippings." The meal was topped off with dandelion, a dish that falls somewhere between being a salad and a vegetable.

Selecting good dandelion from fields, yards, and roadsides is a skill that takes cultivation. As a child, Mother remembers, "I often gathered the dandelion, but my mother often went along because she was particular about cutting off the whole stalk. She didn't want just the individual leaves."

Mother married an expert dandelion scout. "Dad is very good at finding dandelion. He's always been able to see it when it was real young and everybody else would walk around it. You look for fine leaves. We had a lot of it this spring."

The ham-mashed-potatoes-dandelion meal is farmers' fare. "It was one of those meals that made a good aroma and they'd come in hungry from plowing. It took a lot of food for that meal!"

Now retired from the farm, Mother and Dad rarely eat that combination. But dandelion is still a specialty. Grins Mother, "I'm the one who really likes it. Dad will take a little. I'll take a second helping. Then I'll usually take a little bit more!"

Wilted Dandelion

a large bowlful of young dandelion shoots and leaves
6 slices of bacon
1 Tbsp. vinegar
1 Tbsp. flour
1½ Tbsp. sugar
1/4-1/2 cup water

Pull the dandelion leaves off their stalks and chop the leaves. Drop them in a pot of boiling water. Let stand for 5 to 10 minutes. Then drain leaves, pouring off juice.

Brown the bacon. Remove from drippings and crumble. Set aside. Add vinegar, flour, sugar, and water to the drippings. Cook until thickened. Then add bacon.

Pour warm dressing over wilted dandelion and serve.

Makes 4 servings

Ira and Ruth Good got their freezer in 1950. By then they had four boys and a farm. So before they bought a freezer their meat was either canned, smoked or fresh. Or kept in a frozen food locker they rented in Ephrata, five miles away.

They raised chickens, so from late summer through the fall, and into the early winter months, poultry was on the menu. "Dad would kill the chickens for me early in the morning, often on Saturdays, and then I'd feather them while he was milking. If the boys woke up while I was out, they'd just come down and play."

Mother capitalized on chicken's versatility. "Often I cooked the chicken in my pressure cooker with saffron. It takes a good bit of space to grow saffron. And you have to clean the bed but you can't hoe it. My father used to tend it."

Several favorite ways of serving that tender chicken, flavored with saffron, stand out. "I'd have stewed chicken for Saturday dinner, usually with mashed potatoes and gravy made from the chicken broth. But most of the broth I'd save for a big batch of chicken corn soup for Sunday dinner, especially when the boys were small! Often I would make bologna sandwiches with it, plus salad and fruit, or red beet eggs and a dessert."

Brilliantly red hard-boiled eggs bring color and zest to any lunch or dinner table. Some daring cook with a distaste for waste discovered that the juice from cooking red beets could be pickled and used to flavor hardcooked eggs. The Good farm was abundant in eggs and red beets. So Mother made them often. In spite of that, they're still a specialty.

Merle and I and our two daughters go through a routine on our way to Mother and Dad Good's house for a meal. About ten minutes from their home we begin, "What do you think Grandma's going to serve?" Invariably, Merle wishes for ham loaf or oyster filling!

Mother has a sense of timing (I've often wondered how conscious she is of it!) which is very effective. She never wears out a dish. She doesn't serve the favorites everytime! So she keeps us coming—for surprises, and the old specialties.

Oyster filling is a dish worth making into a tradition. Mother remembers, "We had it at my home and Dad had it at his. And I helped make it for one of Dad's brother's or sister's weddings.

"It was a winter dish. My father used to get a lot of oysters in shells, then we'd take them out and use them mostly in soup. But

13

we would have oyster filling for Christmas or special meals."

I made some for the holidays this year. It's a custom I'd like to continue.

Oyster Filling

Some recipes adapt easily to your family's taste. **Oyster Filling** allows for a lot of adjustments, both to taste preferences and the size of the crowd at your table.

Mother Good cooks for two or twenty-two ("I can set a table for eighteen in the dining room," she used to say when they were on the farm.) with almost equal ease. Consequently her **Oyster Filling** recipe has never been pinned down to precise quantities. This is her procedure:

white bread, sliced
butter or margarine
oysters with their liquid
milk
salt and pepper

"Cut the bread up into 1/2 to 3/4 inch squares, including the crusts, the day before making the filling so it dries out a little. Put the cubes in a dishpan and cover it with a tea towel.

"The next day melt some butter or margarine in a large pan. Then add the bread cubes to it. Pour additional melted butter over the top. Stir the mixture constantly over the heat until the bread browns, not burns.

"Take a long shallow pan and cover the bottom of it with a layer of the browned bread cubes. Follow that with a layer of oysters (either whole or cut up) that have been warmed in butter; then another layer of bread and another layer of oysters.

"Then pour the oyster liquid mixed with some milk over the whole pan. The filling should be *damp* throughout, not soggy or wet. Add more milk if it seems too dry or more bread if it's gotten too wet. Salt and pepper to taste.

"Bake the dish at 275°-300° until it's heated through (stir it up to check) and slightly browned on top."

Before ham loaf, there was meat loaf. "At first we'd grind up celery and carrots and onions with it. It didn't get as nice as hamburger now because it didn't get as fine. Later we got the butcher to do that."

Even meat loaf had a seasonal aspect. "We'd often have it after the chickens were gone. I'd make it for Sunday dinner, baking it while we were at church. We'd eat scalloped potatoes with it or macaroni and cheese or new potatoes with brown butter, depending on the time of year.

"Ham loaf came much later. I learned about it from other women, fifteen or twenty years ago. It became available in stores and was pretty much of a 'company' dish." It's still a treat.

Ham Loaf

3 lbs. ground ham loaf mix
 (1/4 pork, 1/2 ham, 1/4 beef)
1/2 cup minute tapioca
2 cups milk
1 cup bread crumbs
2 eggs
1 small onion, chopped fine
1/2 tsp. salt

Mix tapioca and milk. Add bread crumbs and let mixture soak for 10 minutes. Combine ham loaf mix, eggs, onion, and salt. Add milk mixture and combine thoroughly. Form into two loaves.

Bake covered at 225° for 3 hours. Uncover; glaze if desired, and bake 1/2 hour more. Cut into 1/2 inch slices for serving.

Glaze

3/4 cup unsweetened pineapple juice
3/4 cup honey
1/2 tsp. prepared mustard

Cook until thickened. Cool. Then spread over loaves.

Makes 10-12 servings

In fact, some years ago when we were planning our wedding reception, Merle's choice of meat was ham loaf. We risked having the caterer prepare it, although it was a first for him. I think Merle decided it was an apt bridge from Mother's meals to someone else's. He did confide to me, after becoming my husband, that he had had a few moments of worry about giving up his mother's cooking for mine.

But to both their credits, neither one has ever corrected my cooking. Mother has even asked for a few of my recipes!

3 Food for the Soul

Sometimes food feeds the soul as well as the body.

When Lena Beiler was a young girl, sent to work in the fields, coming in to eat chased her hunger and her chills. "We would be out husking corn and we'd work until dark. Then we'd come in and Mother would have the fire lit and the meal started. Although it was cornhusking time there were still tomatoes. The house smelled and felt so good!"

The food was simple; often there was no meat on those particular evenings. But her mother was there, and the dishes were filled with Lena's specialty. "I always loved fried potatoes with tomato sauce to put on them. My grandmother knew I liked this, too, and she'd fix it for me if I went to help her or was there visiting."

Lena carried the recipes in her memory when she left home to start her own, but the warmth that always surrounded those dishes was missing. "When we got married and moved to a big farm, cornhusking was one time when I really missed my mother. I'd be out in the cornfield and it would be cool. Then I'd come in and there was no fire. There was no meal cooking. I had to do all that. I had to start everything."

Lena grew up in a resourceful world. "I remember we painted our whole bolognas with wax to preserve them. We had no refrigeration so we buried pork ribs in fat and put eggs for baking in lime water." Although Lena no longer needs to channel her best ideas into those kinds of efforts, her background gave her energy and ingenuity to last a lifetime.

Despite the fact that her family is gone from home, Lena Beiler still plants a big garden. The plenty it yields she shares with her daughters, their husbands, and children, and the many guests she serves from her Amish Mennonite church.

Lena is on the grandmother end of things now. She and Christ, who died a few years ago, had six daughters and they're all married. But that doesn't mean Lena's been left behind. The girls, their husbands, and children are all within shouting distance. Lena sees her brood constantly. In the summer they can and freeze together, in the winter they quilt together, visit friends and relatives in rest homes, or paper each other's living rooms!

Tomato Sauce

**1 quart canned tomatoes or
or tomato juice cocktail
3 Tbsp. flour
2-3 Tbsp. water
4 Tbsp. brown sugar**

Heat tomatoes or juice to the boiling point. Stir flour and water together to make a paste. Then add the paste and sugar to the hot tomatoes, stirring until the sauce thickens.

Makes 6 servings

But then, that's not unusual. As a child, Lena's grandparents were inseparable from her world. Her Grandmother Smoker was an expert pear butter maker. She did it "by feel," of course. "Grussmommy would come the night before and we'd all peel pears. Baskets of them," Lena remembers. "Then the next morning Dauddy would bring Grussmommy over while the men were still milking. She wanted to get those pears started cooking in our big copper kettle. We had a big wooden paddle to stir with, so the pears wouldn't scorch."

It was an all-day affair. "When the pears got soft we put them through the fruit press." That smoothed the sauce. "Then we poured it back into the copper kettle and added 100 pounds of sugar. The sauce just boiled and boiled for several hours. Somebody had to stir it constantly or it would burn. When it had boiled down, Grussmommy would test it with a spoon to see if it had reached a jelly-like consistency," Lena remembers.

It was the moment for a skilled judgment. If Grussmommy decided it was right, into the crocks it went. Lena pictures the line-up of crocks. "They had all been warmed—quarts, two-quarts, and

18

gallons. After they were filled we took bread wrappers, cut them to fit the top of the crocks, dipped the wrappers in water, then put them down on top of the butter. We didn't have waxed paper then."

The butter was doubly sealed. "Next we took newspapers or brown paper and fit it down over the top and outside of the crocks. Then we cut rubber bands from inner tubes and tied them tightly around the paper. That pear butter would keep for a whole year. It didn't get moldy and stingy." A labor-intensive project, but unsurpassed in the flavor and embrace it yielded.

In Lancaster County the Old Order Amish hold their church services in members' homes. "I always liked to go to Dauddy Smokers for church," Lena smiles. Relatives, neighbors, and friends were invited to stay for supper. "Grussmommy never knew how many people she'd have, but she usually made caramel pudding! I loved it with ground peanuts on top. I can still see Dauddy sitting there, shelling the peanuts for on top. Grussmommy always served it cold."

Caramel Pudding

2 Tbsp. butter
3/4 cup brown sugar
1 quart milk
2 eggs
2 Tbsp. cornstarch
2 Tbsp. flour
pinch of salt
1/4 cup milk
chopped peanuts

Melt the butter in a heavy saucepan. Add the brown sugar and stir until brown. Stir in 1 quart milk and warm; then set aside.

Beat together eggs, cornstarch, flour, salt, and 1/4 cup milk. Add to the warm milk and stir just until it reaches the boiling point. Remove from heat and beat with a rotary beater. Cool; then cover top with chopped fresh peanuts before serving.

Variation: line serving dish with buttered graham cracker crumbs. Dip in half the pudding. Add a layer of buttered graham cracker crumbs; then the remaining pudding. Top with whipped cream and dust with graham cracker crumbs.

4 Sturdy Food for a Big Brood

When Sharon Clymer Landis talks about her favorite foods she also talks about family. For she's always been surrounded by "tribe." She is the eighth in a family of eleven children. And when she and Jay got married, they moved to his parents' farm, making their home in one end of the giant stone house. On the other side live Jay's folks. Jay shares the potato farming with his dad. "In the summer," explains Sharon, "we often eat together after the men come in from the fields."

Reflecting on her childhood, Sharon smiles, "We were always together for meals. Mom would have us all awake before Dad went to work. I just remember the long table with all of us around it."

One breakfast food stands out—banana milkshakes! "Because there were so many of us, money was handled pretty carefully. Bananas were a real treat. They were bought for the people who went to work—and we poor little kids who stayed home would pest and pest Mom until she'd finally make us a milkshake!" Mrs. Clymer put one or two very ripe bananas, four cups of milk, one-fourth cup brown or white sugar or honey, and a teaspoon of vanilla in the blender and mixed it for two minutes. In that form one or two bananas would feed five or six hungry mouths.

The Clymer clan, in spite of its size, was well fed. "Daddy cared about nutrition," Sharon comments, "so he wanted us to fill up on good stuff. He liked to garden and made us eat all the vegetables he grew. If we took the skins off our potatoes, he'd have fits!"

Not only was every meal preparation a big task, summer food

Food means family for Sharon Landis. She and her ten brothers and sisters were fed solid and basic meals. As enjoyable as the food was the fact that the children and their parents almost always ate together. Sharon's husband is a farmer, so their gardening and food preserving is another family experience. Sharon and Jay belong to a suburban Lancaster Conference Mennonite Church.

21

preservation was a major endeavor. "When we did corn and cut it off for freezing we always knew we'd have corn fritters that evening for supper. We had a big griddle that stretched across two stove burners and you could make six or eight fritters at a time. When we do corn now we save some for fritters that evening. I get hungry for them."

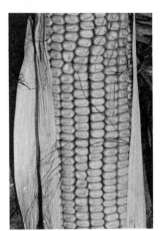

Corn Fritters

2 eggs, separated
4 Tbsp. flour
1/2 tsp. baking powder
1/2 tsp. salt
dash of pepper
1 Tbsp. milk
1 tsp. sugar
2 cups freshly grated or frozen corn,
    blended slightly
oil or butter for frying

Beat egg whites until stiff. Set aside. Beat egg yolks, flour, baking powder, salt, pepper, milk, and sugar and add to the grated corn. Mix thoroughly. Fold in egg whites.

Drop by spoonfuls into greased frying pan. Turn when golden brown on bottom; then brown top. Serve warm with syrup.

Makes 4 servings

"We all loved soup," Sharon says about her brothers and sisters. "I guess that was good because we could get rid of a lot of leftovers!" One favorite was Mortonhouse soup, a hearty vegetable stew, touched off with a little flavoring of cornmeal.

"It was probably a winter dish. And it was special because we could eat all we wanted! Usually our meat was rationed out." Solid and substantial in its ingredients, Mortonhouse soup is a dish that Sharon can serve to Jay, whom she describes as "a farmer who likes his potatoes."

Mortonhouse Soup

1 pound ground beef
1 large onion, chopped
1 cup celery, chopped
1 cup potatoes, diced
1 cup carrots, sliced
salt and pepper to taste
1 pint tomato sauce

2½ quarts water
1/4 cup cornmeal
1/4 cup water

Brown hamburger and onion. In dutch oven combine meat and onion, celery, carrots, potatoes, seasoning, tomato sauce and water. Simmer until the vegetables are tender.

Make a thin paste of the cornmeal and water. Add to soup, stirring constantly until slightly thickened.

Makes 6 servings

Sharon remembers that they seldom had desserts while growing up because her mother didn't have time to bake. There was one dessert, however, that doubled as a meal—deep dish apple dumplings. "Daddy also had an orchard so we had our own apples.

"Mom would put apples in a huge cake pan, quartered and sugared. Then she'd lift a pie crust across the top. It was mostly a summer thing. We ate it warm with milk."

Deep Dish Apple Dumplings

10-12 tart apples, peeled
1 tsp. sugar
1 tsp. cinnamon
3 Tbsp. milk
butter

Slice apples into a buttered 9" x 9" baking dish. Sprinkle with sugar, cinnamon and milk. Dot with butter.

Crust
2 cups flour
1 tsp. salt
2/3 cup shortening
4 Tbsp. boiling water
2 Tbsp. sugar

Measure flour and salt into mixing bowl. Cut in shortening. Sprinkle with hot water and mix until moistened, and dough holds together. Some of the dough will remain crumbly. Reserve that for topping.

Roll out dough that holds together and place on top of sliced apples. Cut slits in crust to allow steam to escape. Add 2 Tbsp. sugar to reserved crumbs and sprinkle on top of crust.

Bake at 400°, 20-30 minutes or until the apples are soft and the crust is browned. Serve hot with milk, cream, or topped with ice cream.

Makes 4-6 servings

5 Keeping Snitz Pie and Chow Chow

Lois Weidman lived a quiet life as the only child of a farm couple. But those years of calm routine are only a memory now!

It all changed when she married Myron Dietz and he brought his jovial and buoyant style to the Weidman farmstead. Lois and Myron started housekeeping at her home. In fact, they still live in the place. Along the way the older Weidmans moved farther out the lane, but within shouting distance, to be handy to help with the farmwork and the little Dietzes.

If she was lonely as a youngster, Lois always had church with its mix of social activities to anticipate. The Weidmans and Dietzes belong to the Old Order River Brethren, a part of the same faith family that includes the Amish, Mennonites, and Brethren in Christ. Small and far-flung, the group maximizes its Sunday meetings together. After church, members and their children share the noon meal and most of the rest of the day. The River Brethren have no church buildings and so meet in members' homes. Preparations for their turn at hosting church gave Lois some taste of her life to come! And she remembers helping her mother to cook for threshing gangs and weekend company.

Today, Lois Dietz's household hums. She and Myron are the parents of six (three of the children live away from home most of the time), and they are hosts to countless visitors. Gregarious schoolteacher Myron brings students and friends home frequently. Church members from their own and other fellowships drop in regularly. If need be they just keep stretching the kitchen table until

24

Lois Dietz cooks with equal grace for two or twenty-two. It's fortunate, since each day may bring surprise guests, helpers on their truck farm, and a fluctuating number of her and Myron's own children to the table. A member of the Old Order River Brethren, Lois has grown to expect feeding company from their scattered fellowships.

25

it reaches the full length of their kitchen and dining room.

Lois greets warm weather guests with iced tea made from her own mix. Even a cautious tea drinker gets a glass with her gentle urging to try it! It's the touch of lemon that gives the tea its special edge, Lois believes. "Myron's mother used to put lemonade in her iced tea. I think that's where I got it," she explains.

Iced Tea

8 bags regular tea
4 bags spearmint or peppermint tea
8 quarts water
2 cups sugar
12 ounces frozen lemonade concentrate

Bring 8 quarts water to a boil. Remove from heat and drop in 12 teabags. Steep for 30 minutes. Stir in the sugar until dissolved. Add frozen lemonade, stirring until it dissolves. Chill and serve.

A people who respect tradition, the River Brethren have let one small custom slide, to the disappointment of the Dietzes—snitz pie! Made from dried apples, the pies were once a given part of the meal that followed Sunday morning church. Lois' mother's version was a favorite of her family's.

"I made up my recipe," says elderly Mrs. Weidman. Her secret? "I put a little lemon juice in." Today the pies are mostly a memory. "Now people just bring in pies, all different kinds. I think years ago drying apples was a practical thing. It was the best way to keep them," says Lois. The coming of improved cold storage methods brought the end of the snitz pie era.

Snitz Pie

3 heaping cups snitz (dried apple slices)
1 cup sugar
2 Tbsp. lemon juice
1/2 tsp. cinnamon (optional)
2 unbaked 9" double pie shells

Cover snitz with water and let soak over night. Cook just until soft; then force through a sieve. To that mixture add the sugar, lemon juice, and cinnamon, if desired.

Pour into two unbaked pie shells. Cover with a top crust. Seal edges. Bake at 425° for 15 minutes; then at 350° for 30 minutes.

Makes 2 9" pies

If eating good food brings people together, so does its preparation. Chow-chow making goes best with a whole bunch of cooks. "My mother's cousins get together to make chow chow," says Lois. "That and housecleaning are about the only things they get together to do!

"We got our chow chow recipe from my Aunt Elizabeth. She got it in one of the homes where she worked as a nurse, helping mothers of new babies. It has a sweet flavor. A lot of others are too sour. I like it better than any chow chow I've ever eaten," Lois smiles.

Chow Chow

2 quarts and 1 pint raw cauliflower
3 pints raw carrots
2 quarts and 1 pint celery
3½ pints raw green and red peppers
2½ pints raw baby lima beans
3 pints sour pickles
1 heaping quart raw onions
salt to taste

Dice each vegetable into 1/2"-1" chunks. Cook each vegetable separately. Season each with salt. Drain and gently mix all vegetables together.

Syrup

1½ pints vinegar or more
1 pint juice from cooked celery
5½ lbs. sugar
6 oz. prepared mustard
3 Tbsp. mustard seed
2 tsp. turmeric
1 tsp. celery seed
2 Tbsp. cornstarch mixed with 1 tsp. water

Combine all ingredients. Add the mixed vegetables and heat to the boiling point. Put into canning jars and seal.

6 Stuff a Turkey with a Duck

Sit in Sadie Stoltzfus' kitchen and all seems well. The quietness there is basic and full. Sadie and her family are in touch with the land and live bountifully from it. Her garden sprawls just beyond the window. Her canning shelves, below in the cellar, are loaded.

Most of her know-how came from working with experienced kitchen hands. And her own girls are following in the same way. "I learned a lot from my older sister," says Sadie. "When I was sixteen I went to live with her during the week to help her—and then I really learned. After we were married, I learned a lot from my husband Aaron's mother. She lived close by. My mother was older and didn't come as often. So I'd ask whoever I could about how to do things." (There are no telephones in Old Order Amish homes in Lancaster County.)

"The girls and I like to cook," Sadie explains. "Sometimes they say they'll do it. Sometimes I do it to give them a break." So although the girls in the Stoltzfus family are outnumbered three to six by the boys, they have a teamwork going that keeps anyone from being overburdened.

If summer brings gardening, autumn and winter bring baking. "In the fall when appetites get better, we bake bread. And now for church we use homemade bread. Years ago we bought it. But it's cheaper to make our own. And we help each other so that whoever has church doesn't need to make it all."

The Old Order Amish meet in homes for Sunday morning church. The hosting family supplies the lunch that follows the service with

Sadie Stoltzfus has vegetable soup in the canner. Homemade vegetable soup meets several needs—it's a good way to use up the garden extras, it's a full-bodied meal anytime, and it's especially handy when food is called for on short notice. A member of the Old Order Amish, Sadie is used to drop-in family and friends.

the help of their neighboring friends and family.

White Bread

1/2 cup lukewarm water
1 package yeast
1 tsp. sugar
2 cups lukewarm water
1¼ tsp. salt
1/3 cup sugar
1¾ Tbsp. shortening
7-8 cups flour

Dissolve the yeast and sugar in the 1/2 cup lukewarm water. Mix the 2 cups water, salt, sugar, and shortening. Then add the yeast mixture and, gradually, the flour. Knead until smooth and elastic. Place in a greased bowl, cover, and set in a warm place to rise until double.

Punch down. Let rise again. Put in two large loaf pans or three medium ones. Let rise until double again. Bake at 350° for 1/2 hour.

Makes 2 large or 3 medium loaves

Sadie offered her family a turkey with a surprise at Thanksgiving dinner a few years ago. "I always thought turkey was kind of dry and duck was pretty greasy. So I stuffed the duck inside the turkey, and that made the turkey meat more moist. The duck really browns, and you can mix the two meats!"

Roast Turkey with Duck

25 lb. turkey
3 lb. duck
filling

Stuff the duck inside the turkey, or lay the duck beside the turkey in the roast pan if using a smaller turkey. Stuff both the duck and turkey with filling.

Rub the turkey with butter and salt. Add water to a depth of 1/2-1 inch. Cover and bake at 350° allowing 20 minutes per pound, combined weight.

Filling

8 cups bread, cubed
1 cup celery, ground
liver, gizzard, and heart from turkey
    and duck, ground
6 eggs, beaten
salt and pepper to taste

Simmer the ground celery with the ground organ meat until tender. Add salt and pepper to the eggs.

30

Then mix eggs with the bread cubes. Add the other mixture and stir until the filling is moistened.

Cookies are pretty regular fare at the Stoltzfuses. Says Sadie, "We eat them year around. We aren't big pie eaters.

"At Christmastime we bake a lot." Sadie and a friend get together for a day and make about ten different kinds of cookies.

Some cookies are more special than others. Sadie smiles. "Either I take date pinwheels to share with her, or I take the dough to make them. Pinwheels do take time. I used to have trouble with them. But I learned to make the dough really cold—refrigerate it overnight—and then they'll work." One of those cases where persistence pays off!

Date Pinwheel Cookies

1 cup shortening
2 cups brown sugar
1/2 cup granulated sugar
3 eggs
4-4½ cups flour
1 tsp. salt
1 tsp. baking soda
1 tsp. cinnamon

Cream together the shortening and sugar. Add the eggs and beat until fluffy.

Sift the flour; then add the salt, soda, and cinnamon and sift again. Add the dry ingredients to the creamed mixture, and beat until smooth. Chill dough in the refrigerator for a few hours. Divide the chilled dough into two parts. Roll each 1/4" thick and spread with filling.

Filling

1½ cups dates or raisins, ground
1 cup sugar
1 cup water
1/2 cup nuts, chopped fine

Combine the fruit, sugar, and water and cook until thickened, stirring constantly. Remove from heat and add the nuts. Cool and spread on the rolled dough.

Roll up, jelly-roll fashion and chill thoroughly in the refrigerator. Slice in rings 1/8 inch thick and place on greased cookie sheets, 1 inch apart. Bake at 375° until golden brown.

Makes 3½ dozen cookies.

31

7 Potato Buns and Doughnuts Anytime

"I think cooking is one of my favorite things. I remember watching my mother at work in the kitchen. She was a really good cook, and I guess I learned to like it through osmosis."

Today there are unmistakable parallels between the two women. Joan Gingrich finds herself swinging into the same rhythm as her mother did while kneading yeast dough, and her kitchen table seems to duplicate the squeak of her mother's as she works on it.

"Although I'm the oldest girl with two younger sisters and one older brother, my mother never left me in charge exactly," Joan (pronounced "Joanne") remembers. "She and I worked together." And for teaching the how-to and love of yeast dough, that was a good strategy. Because Joan happily carries on her mother's potato buns' and doughnuts' tradition.

Both the buns and doughnuts have mashed potatoes in their dough. "Mother never made bread. Instead she made these, always mixing them up in the evening, maybe because they used less yeast in those days and it took longer to rise. She would always make a huge bowl of mashed potatoes for supper that evening. Then she'd take out the cups she needed for buns before setting the serving bowl on the table. She was a short woman just like I am, so she would knead the dough on the table because she couldn't reach the counter. The fun of watching her mix these was as great as the actual eating!"

If one thinks of a favorite food, back come all the attendant memories—smells, sounds, sights! "The smell of yeast was so dis-

Good cooks like to cook, it seems. Joan Gingrich is no exception. She has created her share of food memories for her daughters, as her mother did for her. That legacy includes potato buns and doughnuts. Joan, Jim, and their four daughters are members of a nearby Lancaster Conference Mennonite church.

33

tinctive from anything else Mother made," remembers Joan. "And she kept the buns in a special container in the pantry. We always ate them with molasses. They were so special, we'd just fill ourselves with them when we had them!"

It was no wonder then that Joan Nissley and Jim Gingrich put potato buns on their wedding reception menu. And Mrs. Nissley made them all, enough for their 200 guests! Some years later Joan passed the kindness on when she made the buns for her youngest sister Nancy's wedding day.

Potato Buns and Doughnuts

1 cup sugar
1 cup mashed potatoes
1/2 cup lard or shortening
3 eggs, beaten
1½ tsp. salt
1½-2 packs yeast
1 cup warm water
5 cups flour

Mix together well the sugar, potatoes, lard, eggs, and salt.

Dissolve the yeast in 1 cup warm water; and then add that to the above mixture.

Stir in about 3 cups of flour. Add the remaining 2 cups flour while kneading, kneading until the dough is no longer sticky but moist.

Let rise until doubled.

For Potato Buns:

Roll out dough to a 3/4"-1" thickness. Cut into bun shapes with a jar or doughnut cutter (or clover leaf — or crescent-shaped cutter) and put on greased cookie sheets about 2 inches apart. Let them rise until puffy but not doubled (they should not be touching).

Brush with milk. Bake at 325° until lightly golden brown, about 12 minutes.

Makes about 3 dozen

For Doughnuts:

Roll out dough to a 1/2" thickness. Cut out with a doughnut cutter; then place on clean towels laid over cookie sheets or boards. Let rise until almost double; then fry in fat, heated to 350°-375°, about 4 inches deep. Keep fat at that temperature throughout the frying. Turn doughnuts once while frying, when they turn golden brown.

Makes about 3½ dozen

Doughnut Glaze:

1 lb. 10x sugar
1/2 cup rich milk (or a bit more)
1 Tbsp. soft butter
1 tsp. vanilla

Heat together just until butter is melted and milk is warm. Glaze while doughnuts are hot.

The town of Lititz in northern Lancaster County mounts a Fourth of July extravaganza that brings admirers from miles away. "We lived about two miles west of Lititz," Joan explains, "and our farm was a little higher than the town, so we'd sit in our sloping backyard and watch. My mother's family was from Elizabethtown and they never had fireworks up there, so they'd come down to 'Aunt Martha's.'

"Mother always made doughnuts for the occasion and when it got dark we'd bring them out. It's a little crazy to spend a whole day in July standing over a hot stove, but she did it for the social thing. I think her doughnuts became as attractive as the fireworks! Of course there were no freezers in those days so we had to eat them all the day they were made!

"Mother didn't glaze them until recent years. She used to coat them with granulated sugar and cinnamon. My family doesn't like that as well, but to me there's a certain goodness in that."

Joan and her schoolteacher husband, Jim, have spent many snow days baking buns and doughnuts with their four daughters. Smiles Joan, "I've often said I can't bake them by myself since it makes a big portion and it's a hard thing to keep frying and glazing them while they're still warm. I could manage, but it's so much more fun to do it with a group! And I don't make them on the Fourth of July!"

8 Zwieback are Our Cousins

Katherine Penner Hostetler was born in Russia and then moved with her family to the prairies of Manitoba when she was about a year old. Her cooking today reflects her Russian Canadian Mennonite heritage.

Most of our people have borrowed from the food traditions they've lived closest to. No less so the Russian Mennonites whose history of much migration from the Netherlands to Prussia to the Soviet Union to midwestern Canada and the United States is reflected in their traditional menus.

Many of their particular foods are different from Pennsylvania Dutch dishes, but they are cousins in quality: hearty, peasant-like, from the earth, many times utterly simple, yet richly filling.

Touch Kathy Hostetler's "food nerve," and back flow sweet and sad memories. "We were five children. We lived on a farm in the country. I was the oldest. And among all the struggles, the children came. There were times that seemed so difficult. But I guess my parents had the right resource." The Great Depression fell during the twenty years Kathy lived on the Manitoba prairies. And her immigrant family was beaten about by the trouble of those times.

"Now I think of the food we ate as special. In those days we sometimes turned up our noses at it! We had 'English' neighbors and we were somewhat friendly to each other. Then there were hints that maybe we should have them over for a meal. I was so worried about what Mother would make. I knew there was no way our food would mesh into their life. I was just glad when the epi-

Kathy Hostetler makes Russian Mennonite food in Pennsylvania Dutch Country! There are others in her Mennonite congregation who also have roots in Canada, Prussia, and Russia, but Kathy's zwieback are still a tasty curiosity to most native Lancaster County cooks!

sode was over!"

There are basics to this diet. "Every Saturday Mother would bake zwieback—that means 'two bakes'; there were two parts to the bun. They were for late afternoon or evening coffee when guests came on Sunday. You just knew wherever you went visiting, there would be zwieback."

There was butter available for making zwieback, but spreading it on the finished buns was an extravagance! "Jam was okay. Only guests were allowed to put butter on!"

"Dad would just say to Mother on the way home from church that he had invited so-and-so for Faspa (coffee hour). And she wasn't worried. I like that!

"It wasn't until the last few years that I started baking zwieback. Mother would visit us and see my zwieback and couldn't believe that I had made them! As children we would sit around and watch her preparing them. She was usually in a hurry. She would pinch off the pieces of dough, and if we asked to try, she'd say, 'Well, maybe another day.' That day never came. I guess she learned from watching her mother, and she figured I would too. Now I bake them regularly!"

Kathy's husband, John, is from Ohio and of the Swiss German Mennonite strain, so zwieback entered his life only when Kathy did. Despite that, he eats them, enjoys them, and their two grown sons, Rich and Bob, do also.

Zwieback

2 cups milk
1 cup shortening
2 tsp. salt
4 Tbsp. sugar
1 yeast cake
2 tsp. sugar
1 cup lukewarm water
2 eggs, beaten
8-10 cups flour, sifted

Scald the milk. To it add the shortening, salt, and 4 Tbsp. sugar.

In another bowl, crumble the yeast; then add 2 tsp. sugar and the lukewarm water to it. Put aside in a warm place until spongy.

Add the yeast mixture and eggs to the milk which has cooled to lukewarm. Mix well and gradually stir in the flour. Then knead the dough until it is soft and smooth.

Cover and let rise in a warm place until double. Pinch off small pieces of dough the size of a walnut. Place one inch apart on a greased cookie sheet. Pinch off slightly smaller balls and place on top of the bottom balls. Push down so they're secure. Let rise again until doubled.

Bake at 400-425° for 15-20 minutes.

Makes about 4 dozen

And there were other foods. "Verenike was a favorite of ours, I guess because we just grew up with it. Mother would make them for my birthday meal when I was a youngster. Someone new would have to develop a taste for it. It's not that tantalizing or attractive, but for my parents in Russia, it was something filling. In the days of the Revolution people worked hard."

Verenike are little dough pockets stuffed with cottage cheese, which are dropped into water and boiled for several minutes.

Kathy remembers, "They're a lot of work. You should serve them with a smoked ham or sausage with gravy. And that's it—no salad or vegetable. We just ate all the verenike we could. Sometimes my mother would fill them with sour cherries or rhubarb instead of cottage cheese. And when they were left over, she would brown them in a skillet. I've just shied away from making them, because they're so much work, but maybe one of these days . . . !"

Some familiar dishes are worth remembering more for the mirror they are to immigrant farming life than the pleasure they brought in eating! "Mother usually made bubbat in the winter when the cookstove was going anyhow. I was never real keen on it.

"Bubbat was simply a batter. She'd take home-cured smoked sausage and lay it in the skillet, then pour the batter over it and let it bake. When it was finished she'd slice it into squares and we'd eat just that. Sometimes we'd put syrup over it or jam if we had it, but that was a luxury."

Kathy has cherished memories of noodle-making and noodles themselves. "Very often on the day that we washed—and that was an all-day affair—Mother would make noodles. She'd do it on the kitchen table, stacking thin layers of dough. Then with her knife she would snip, snip, snip so fast and the noodles would go flying!

39

The window was open and the air was warm, and it would dry the noodles. She had us girls to run the washing machine, and the noodles would cook quickly, so I guess that's why she'd make them on that day."

In those times of struggling to survive, noodles stood on their own as a main dish. Mrs. Penner sauteed some onions, thickened them with flour, and then covered them with cream (from their own cows, of course). If there were ham drippings she'd brown the onions in them to add a bit of flavoring. Kathy recalls the procedure, "Then she would put the noodles in a long tray that she brought from Russia—I still have the tray—and pour the gravy over them. And that's how she served it!"

Homemade Egg Noodles

2 cups flour
4 eggs
2 tsp. salt

Sift the flour into a bowl. Make a well and drop the 4 eggs and salt into it. Mix by hand and knead it into a stiff dough.

Divide the dough into 4 balls and roll each out very thin. Lay on a clean cloth to partly dry, but do not allow them to get brittle. Cut each into 2 inch strips. Place 5 or 6 strips on top of each other; then cut with a very sharp knife into fine noodles. Spread them out loosely to dry.

Bring water to boil; then add noodles and a dash of salt. Return to a full rolling boil. Drain the noodles; then rinse with water. Put back into kettle and stir in butter to prevent their sticking and to keep them warm.

Sometimes these noodles turned up in soup. "Homemade chicken noodle soup was something Mother made often. We kids had to chase a chicken, then Mother would behead it and follow through with the process.

"When she was sick for a number of years, she got jars and jars of homemade chicken noodle soup. It's something of a tradition among our people. Mother would often take it to someone who came home from the hospital, maybe if they had a baby."

Chicken Noodle Soup

a whole chicken
2 tsp. salt
10 peppercorns
1 small onion
1 bay leaf
fresh or dried parsley

Cut the chicken into serving pieces. Place in a kettle and add water to cover. Then add the remaining ingredients. Simmer slowly until the chicken is tender. Skim off the fat and add 3 Tbsp. butter. Add homemade noodles that have been cooked separately.

Food stirs memories and for a moment Kathy reflects on what was—and what is. "There was something about bread through the whole Russian experience where bread became almost holy. In those days it was portioned out. It was rich and moist. So when zwieback became stale, Mother would just toast them lightly, so they would keep almost indefinitely. You see, we ate things that weren't absolutely fresh, but it was all right."

The Hostetlers eat heartily, but simply today. They draw on their Russian and Swiss German Mennonite traditions, but also on their careers which have brought them face-to-face with hunger and poverty. Kathy and John met in Germany when Kathy was working with Mennonite Central Committee (MCC), a relief and service organization. Today they live in Akron, Pennsylvania, where John is Material Aid Director for MCC, overseeing their Relief Sales, the processing of donated clothing and blankets, and the MCC canner which prepares food for the needy.

Although at home in richly fertile Lancaster County, Kathy and John Hostetler eat well, yet conscientiously. Thanks to their histories and their commitments.

9 Treat Your Family to Oatmeal Bread

"My oatmeal bread recipe is special to me because of the person I got it from," smiles Naomi Stoltzfus. "One Saturday morning my husband and I and three single friends took two teams of horses the eighteen miles to Lebanon where another friend and her husband lived. We had eaten a light breakfast and when we got there we were really hungry and she was baking bread. No sooner had we gotten there than she took it out of the oven, sliced it and served it to us warm, spread with butter and jelly. It got us off to a really good visit!"

A warm memory can be powerful enough to create a tradition. Naomi carried the recipe home and now makes the bread as part of her family's regular diet. Not only did the recipe produce delicious bread, it connected with her impulse to eat healthfully. "Now that I make oatmeal bread, we don't even have white bread. Sometimes for our meal after church there is white and dark bread and our children will choose the brown! You can train yourself to eat certain ways. If you stop eating desserts, pretty soon you don't miss them."

Naomi isn't on a campaign; she simply is disciplined in her eating and cooking. Although a member of the Old Order Amish, a people known for their rich and heavy foods, Naomi finds some traditional eating habits changing. Desserts, for example. The days of serving pie, cake, a couple of puddings, and ice cream all at the same meal are passing. It's still done, but less frequently. "The friends I feel closest to are mostly schoolteachers, and they feel as

In Naomi Stoltzfus' kitchen stands a space heater. But it does more than just heat the room. "In the winter I put a frozen piece of meat on the cook top and it's done by lunchtime. Our potatoes I bake in the coal hopper," she explains.

I do about food," Naomi explains. "So when I have them for a meal I prepare a simple dessert, usually pie and ice cream."

"Butchering has changed," Naomi points out. "My dad said when he was a boy, they'd figure that one pig would be enough to feed two adults for a year. (Of course, they'd eat beef and chicken also!) But now there's less eating of pork and ham. And, in general, we just don't eat as much meat as we used to."

Naomi was a schoolteacher for eight years. That was the beginning of her exposure to careful eating. That job also took her out of the kitchen. Now with three preschoolers, cooking three meals each day, and doing dishes three times a day, "I get a little bogged down sometimes," she confesses. "But my husband likes to eat the way I do—a lot of raw foods, few snacks and desserts." Furthermore, she likes to sew. "I enjoy baking but I don't want to do it two or three times a week. Maybe every other week. I'd sooner sit at the sewing machine and make pillows. Then you have something to show for it, too!"

So when Naomi plans a baking day, she makes it worthwhile. "Usually I bake six loaves of bread at a time and freeze four." That stretches into a good many suppers of soup and sandwiches. (The Stoltzfuses eat their main meal at noon because they're all at home, and they feel better that way.)

Oatmeal Bread

2 cups boiling water
1 cup dry rolled oats
2 Tbsp. yeast
1/3 cup lukewarm water
1 Tbsp. salt
½ cup honey
1 egg
1 tsp. vinegar
2 Tbsp. blackstrap molasses
2 cups whole wheat flour
4-5 cups white flour

Pour boiling water over dry oats. Let stand 30 minutes. Meanwhile, dissolve yeast in lukewarm water.

To first mixture add the salt, honey, egg, vinegar, molasses, and yeast mixture. Gradually add enough flour so the dough can be kneaded. (Dough should be slightly sticky.) Knead 5-10 minutes.

Let rise until double in size, about 1 hour. Punch down, then divide into 2 or 3 loaves. Let rise again.

Bake at 350° for 25-30 minutes.

Makes 2 or 3 loaves

"I like to use my own tomato cocktail juice for tomato soup," says Naomi. Made from their homegrown plum tomatoes, the juice is pulpy and so thick, "you don't need to add flour when making soup or many crackers when you eat it. You just spoon it up!"

Tomato Soup

1 pint tomato juice cocktail
scant ¼ cup water
  ("Just enough to rinse out the jar!")
⅛ tsp. baking soda
¼ cup milk

Heat juice and water to the boiling point. Stir soda in carefully, watching that the mixture doesn't boil over.

Add milk and heat, but don't boil.

Tomato Juice Cocktail

½ bushel tomatoes
3 stalks celery (leaves and all)
3 large onions
6 medium carrots
3 green peppers
a little water
1 cup sugar
2 Tbsp. salt

Cut raw vegetables into 1 inch pieces. Put all together into large stockpot. Add water to a depth of 1 inch. Cook slowly until soft, then put through food press.

To pureed mixture add sugar and salt. Bring to a boil. Pour into jars and seal.

10 Creative Tampering

Leon Stauffer likes food. "I'm not a woodcarver. I can't paint. I just don't have that natural talent. But there's something I like about food and creating something beyond the recipe! I know my way around the kitchen because I've always had to help."

And now he enjoys cooking as a break from the office. Leon is Executive Secretary of the Eastern Mennonite Board of Missions in Salunga, Pennsylvania, and Executive Secretary of the Board of Congregational Resources of Lancaster Mennonite Conference. What's more, cooking is his way of relieving Nancy, who is a part-time bookkeeper, of some housework and the care of their three children.

Leon's kitchen experience started early and of necessity. The last in a family of four, he was eight years younger than his next older brother. When he was eight years old, his mother died.

"The thing that's so vivid to me was the year my sister came home from college (Eastern Mennonite in Harrisonburg, Virginia) so she could help at home. We would do dishes together. She'd wash and I'd dry and we'd prop a hymnbook up at the window at the sink. She taught me to sing new songs, and also to sing in parts. I especially remember 'My God, I Thank Thee.'

"When my sister wasn't there, my dad would shut things off early, out in the fields, to come in and fix lunch."

Leon, the fledgling cook, was in the right setting to do a little experimenting. And his creative tampering has continued! "I don't know why I can't let a taste be a taste," he smiles. "I need to

Leon Stauffer works around the kitchen because he just can't quite help it! A church executive at the Eastern Mennonite Board of Missions and Lancaster Conference Board of Congregational Resources, Leon finds relief in sauteéing mushrooms and putting the extras on a tossed salad. A gardening break may make knotty church matters a bit more manageable!

47

accentuate it somehow. When I perk coffee, I sprinkle a little salt over it! I like to make the frills. I'll go to some lengths to stir-fry onions and mushrooms to sprinkle on a salad. Nancy gets fed up with me adding seasonings to dishes that we already know are good!"

Food—whether making it, smelling it, or chewing it—is a sensual experience for Leon. "I just really enjoy the odors. Sometimes I like the aroma almost more than the eating!"

On the other hand, he won't deny the pleasure of eating! "I like to eat something with body to it. When I make pancakes I sprinkle sunflower or sesame seeds on them. Something crunchy. And when I make soup I put something in it that snaps when you bite it. I do that for salads, too."

Leon claims not to make many meals from start to finish. "Usually I assist. I'll often get the colds things ready." But at least once a year he makes the family a feast. And on that day he delights in the atmosphere as much as the food. "New Year's Day is usually a time when it's just our family together. I almost always make sauerkraut and spare ribs for that first day of the year. It's part of a splurge for us since we don't eat that much meat.

"I like to get that pork going so it steams up the windows and you can't see out. The smell is there. It's like all the good things are inside. I'm away from the office; there are no deadlines."

Oh yes, any cook who tried Leon's pork and sauerkraut recipe is invited to make their own additions to it. Because he does! "When I make it, I add a little brown sugar to the meat and sauerkraut about halfway through the cooking time."

Pork and Sauer/Sweet Kraut

2 lbs. spare ribs, cut into 3 or 4 pieces
salt and pepper to taste
dash of sugar
water
1¾ lb. can sauerkraut
3 Tbsp. brown sugar
¼ cup onion, diced
1 apple, peeled and sliced thin

Season the meat, then brown slowly in a heavy skillet. Add water to a depth of ½-1 inch. Cover and cook slowly one hour.

Spread sauerkraut over pork. Sprinkle with brown sugar, onion, and apple. Cover and cook slowly one more hour.

Makes 4 servings

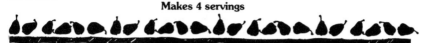

The Stauffers are a family with a food conscience, shaped partly by their exposure to poverty during a year of service in the Philippines. And so some international flavor has crept into their Pennsylvania Dutch diet. It's a venture that has pleased Leon. "With Filipino cooking, I like both the food and the procedure. With stir-frying there's a certain art to knowing when to put the carrots and onions and meat in to get them the right degree of tenderness.

"We never eat adobo without remembering our experiences overseas. We talk about our Filipino friends. We remember that they have mostly vegetables while we have excess meat in our adobo."

Adobo

1½ lb. fresh pork cubes
2-4 Tbsp. vinegar
2 Tbsp. soy sauce
1 tsp. salt
3 cloves garlic, minced
1 small bay leaf
¼ tsp. pepper
1 Tbsp. sugar
½ cup water
2 Tbsp. cooking oil

Combine all ingredients, except oil, in a pot and let stand for at least 30 minutes. Then simmer for 1 hour or until the meat is tender. Drain and reserve sauce.

Heat cooking oil in skillet. Brown pork on all sides. Transfer to serving dish.

Pour off remaining oil from skillet. Add reserved sauce and cook for a minute or two, scraping all browned bits of meat from pan. Pour sauce over meat and serve.

Makes 4 servings

11 A Hennely Mose Breakfast or Cabbage Supper

Marian Lapp's brother Sam says she's one of the best cooks he knows! Marian, who lives with her husband and five of their seven children (the two oldest daughters are married) on a large farm between Intercourse and Gap, manages a sizeable garden and helps with raising seven acres of cabbage each year. "Oh, we just eat simply," she smiles. "I don't put a lot of time into making fancy dishes. I make food that doesn't take a lot of time in preparation, at least on an everyday basis. We *can* do special things if it's a special time!"

Because the Lapps are on a farm, Marian has family to feed three meals each day. With the care of her children and responsibilities outdoors, she's learned to squeeze in the cooking and rely on help from her daughters when they're home from school. "At noon we'll have sandwiches and soup. The evening meal is our warm meal and we eat that pretty early, before the milking. While I do the kitchen clean-up after supper, the others do the barn chores. So we're all done about the same time."

The Lapp sons and daughters know they're needed at home. They help happily—and almost effortlessly.

How do parents inspire children to pitch in? Were the children always so willing? "It was a struggle when they were younger." Marian recalls. "Our eight-year-old has definite chores to do. But he'd just as soon get out of them or any extra jobs. But we don't hear that from our fifteen-year-old anymore. I guess it's just the process of maturing."

50

Although the Lapps sell most of their cabbage, they eat it often and enjoy it. Marian's "Three Layer Dinner," with cabbage as a main ingredient, is a favorite with her own family and guests. "Children like it, too," she smiles.

Raising seven acres of cabbage is a Lapp family project. Traditionally, many Old Order groups grow tobacco as a cash crop and as a way of involving their children in productive work. The Lapps, who belong to the Weavertown Amish Mennonite Church, prefer growing food.

Marian speaks with quiet conviction. "I think it's very much a part of our heritage to *enjoy* working, not doing it just because you have to. We think it's important to work *with* our children. They learn well that way. The girls work in the kitchen much the way I do. They see me do it. And the boys in the barn see their father work and do much as he does."

So that explains the cabbage fields. The Lapps call it their "family project." "We've been farming cabbage ever since we were married," Marian explains. And when the children grew old enough to help, it brought the family not only income, but productive togetherness.

Here's how it works. "The men get the field ready in the early spring. Then from mid-April until the end of July we plant. Planting takes four people—one to drive the tractor and three to ride on the back to set the plants in the ground. Every week, April through July, we put out between four and five thousand plants. Aaron and the boys do the irrigation, cultivation, and spraying.

"Then at the end of June or the beginning of July we go out cutting. All the cabbage is cut by hand. We go out several days a week, then, for only an hour or two each time. That's how long it takes to cut a wagon load.

"All of us help with the cutting except the two youngest ones. But the little ones go along out and ride in the wagon and sometimes take a nap. They've all done that! Or Cynthia likes to run along in the rows and pick the wildflowers."

The Lapps contract with wholesalers who buy their cabbage for resale, or they sell directly to local restaurants. At Thanksgiving they wrap it up for the year.

"Sometimes the cabbage business becomes tiresome, but we don't stick with it that long at a time. And we all work together," reflects Marian. "Cabbage—and work—is just an accepted part of our schedule and life. As the children grow older they don't complain."

Marian claims not to be an innovative cook. "My husband's a meat and potatoes man, so that's mostly what I cook! We have our own beef cattle here, so we eat a good bit of roast beef. Baked potatoes or mashed potatoes go with that. We're a great mashed potatoes family!

"Or we have meat loaf and scalloped potatoes. They definitely go together since the family usually wants gravy with their potatoes. And meat loaf doesn't make any and scalloped potatoes don't need any!"

But despite sticking to simple basic food, she's concocted a dish that makes her daughters hungry as she describes how to make it. "A lot of people say they don't like cabbage. But when I serve 'Three Layer Dinner' they say it's really good. They aren't sure what they're eating! And children like it, too."

It's a main dish that can be prepared ahead, then left to bake if the cook needs to be away before mealtime. "If I know I'm going to be gone until right before dinner, I can get this ready to go in the oven while I'm outside," Marian explains.

Three Layer Dinner

1½ lb. hamburger
salt and pepper to taste
¼ cup ketchup
1 head of cabbage
6-8 cups potatoes, diced
salt and pepper to taste
4 slices cheese
1½ cups milk

Brown hamburger, then season with salt and pepper. Mix in ketchup. Set aside.

Shred ½ head of raw cabbage into a baking dish. Add half of raw diced potatoes. Sprinkle with salt and pepper. Add all of hamburger mixture. Cover with slices of cheese.

Shred remaining cabbage and sprinkle over cheese. Add remaining raw diced potatoes. Pour 1½ cups milk over all. Bake at 375° for 1½-2 hours.

Makes 6-8 servings

Things slow down on the farm during the winter. Then there's time for a Hennely Mose breakfast.

Hennely Mose is a dried beef omelet named after two bachelor brothers who supposedly invented the recipe. Who they were and how the dish became part of the Lapp family's menu is a mystery.

"We don't know where it came from," Marian smiles. "Likely it's from my mother-in-law's mother. And it's possible other people

54

eat it, too, but call it something else. We always eat it for breakfast, but it wouldn't have to be limited to that."

A special tradition has grown up around the dish. Once a year in the wintertime Aaron's five brothers and sisters and their spouses come to Cider Mill Farm for a Hennely Mose breakfast. Marian and Aaron host the event since they live on the home farm. But Aaron's mother makes the omelet. "None of us can make it like she does," explains Marian.

It's a time for memories and adult visiting. "We usually do it on a weekday morning when the children are in school. It's more of a leisurely way to eat together than when all the little ones are along. We did it once and found we liked it pretty good, so we just sort of kept it up!"

Marian supplies the rest of the meal. "We have homefried potatoes with Hennely Mose and toast and coffee. We like the omelet with ketchup on it. The children, when they have it, especially like it with ketchup!"

Hennely Mose

4 Tbsp. margarine
1/4 lb. chipped dried beef
3 eggs
3 heaping Tbsp. flour
1½ cups milk

Melt margarine; then brown dried beef in it. Beat together the eggs and flour. Add milk.

Pour egg and milk mixture into hot skillet over dried beef. Stir up frequently until the mixture is moist and fluffy, not dry.

Makes 4 servings

Note: If you want to make more servings, prepare them in separate batches, rather than doubling or tripling portions.

The sprawling farm is rich with fresh food for the Lapps and others and full of at least three generations of memories. Marian and Aaron, with the help of their children, work hard at cultivating both the land and the stories.

12 Food from the Land and the Depression

May Frey likes throwing herself into big company meals. It's the little ones that stump her, she claims! Now there's an irony somewhere in that confession, just as there seems to be another hidden in her statement, "I'm not a creative cook. You ought to see my cookbook collection. Maybe I'm still trying to teach myself to cook!" Instead it sounds like modesty, coming from a woman who goes on to say, "I'd sooner bake—bread, pies, and cakes. And when we have Fresh Air kids here, we bake a lot of cookies."

It seems that May the cook believes that if you're going to mess up the kitchen, you ought to make it worthwhile. Have fun. Do it right.

May Fisher Frey comes from a line of schoolteachers. Her grandmother was one; so was her mother. From them she learned independence and grit, and how one manages a home, family, and career without skimping on the food. She needed every bit of that know-how when she became a nurse and, after marrying Emerson, the mother of four sons and one daughter. She had joined a business freundschaft; Emerson is the treasurer of a large family-owned dairy.

May's home was a farm in central Pennsylvania. Most of her family's food came from their own land. Their recipes were shaped by the Depression. "I remember we had an eggless, milkless, butterless cake. Potato soup with rivels was often a winter evening's meal. We had a house that had high ceilings and was hard to heat, so a supper like that was good."

May Frey reads cookbooks for fun. But some of her favorite recipes are old family hand-me-downs, a few from Depression days. Not only tasty, those foods fit with her nursing know-how and the world food concerns of the Brethren in Christ Church of which she's a member.

Treats came from the garden. "Before freezers, leaf lettuce salad was our first taste of spring. You felt the early warm days of sunshine with the promise of more to come. It's a salad I still make," May smiles.

Leaf Lettuce Salad

a serving bowl full or half a dishpan full of
   cutting lettuce
2 Tbsp. cider vinegar
2 Tbsp. sugar
3/4 cup cream
3 hardboiled eggs, diced
dash of paprika

   Wash and drain lettuce well. Mix vinegar and sugar; then add cream and blend. Pour over the lettuce. Then garnish with the diced egg and sprinkles of paprika.

Makes 4 servings

Early spring also brought strawberries. "The Pennsylvania Railroad tracks ran right through our farm. It was the Mainline. And along those tracks grew the best wild strawberries," May remembers. "Going there was an excursion! When we were younger we weren't supposed to go by ourselves. It was primarily my mother and I who would go. Usually my two brothers were in the fields and my father seldom went."

The railroad tracks held all sorts of possibilities in those days for May. "It made me want to travel!" So she and her mother dreamed. But strawberry picking had its own share of reality and May recalls, "Till you picked enough of those little berries for a family, and then got them ready, you had shot a half a day! They were so tiny, so our shortcake was always a meal and not just dessert."

Although they are tiringly small, wild strawberries have a zestier flavor than tame ones. What's more, they were a send-off to all sorts of imaginary points.

After picking, there was more ceremony! "To serve the shortcake, we always used a long, deep meat platter that had been my great-grandmother's. The meal was really sort of a creation. My mother would first put in a layer of shortcake, then a layer of strawberries, then another layer of cake and strawberries.

"We kind of did two things when we had that shortcake," May reflects. "We talked family history, and we thought of faraway places."

Wild Strawberry Shortcake

2 cups flour
2 tsp. baking powder
1½ Tbsp. sugar
1/2 tsp. salt
4 Tbsp. butter
1 egg, beaten
3/4—1 cup milk

Combine the flour, baking powder, sugar, and salt. Then cut the butter into that mixture until crumbly.

Beat the egg and add the milk to it; then pour over the crumbly mixture. Stir together lightly only until it is all moistened.

Bake at 400° for 20 minutes in a cake or pie pan. Serve warm, covered with wild strawberries.

There was another good cook in May's ancestry whose legacy lives on through her ice box rolls. She was Great Aunt Becky. "Those rolls are still a favorite around here," explains May. "It wouldn't be Christmas without them."

Great Aunt Becky's Ice Box Rolls

1 cup butter
2 cups brown sugar
1/2 cup sour milk or buttermilk
4 3/4 cups flour, sifted 3 times
1 tsp. baking soda, sifted 3 times
2 eggs
1 cup walnuts (black, if possible), chopped

Cream together the butter and brown sugar. Blend in the milk. Sift the flour and baking soda together, 3 times; then mix into the creamed mixture. Add the eggs and chopped walnuts and blend thoroughly.

Form the batter into a long roll on floured waxed paper or aluminum foil. Refrigerate over night. Then slice into 1/4" thick slices and bake at 350° for 12 minutes.

(The batter can be kept in the refrigerator up to two weeks and can be sliced as needed.)

Variation: Chopped dates or candied cherries may also be added to the batter.

13 Keeping It Simple But Good

"My interest in foods has developed over the years. I never really got a kick out of my cooking classes," confesses Elaine Good. But you'd never know it now when you eat at her table!

As a child she first began baking cakes. "I started when I was nine or ten. Then Mother taught me to bake pies, and soon I became the pie baker. One reason I enjoyed it so much was that my older brother always really fussed about how good they were. And they were usually apple pies.

"When Leon and I got married, he said, 'If you're going to use your time making pies, don't waste it on anything but apple!' I don't know where my recipe came from. I think maybe my grandmother taught my mother.

"The first year we were married, Leon's brother, Merle, was also a student at Eastern Mennonite College in Harrisonburg, Virginia. He and I made a deal: he would buy a whole basket of apples and we could keep some of the apples if I'd make him pies. I was thrilled! We did that a couple of times that fall and winter."

Elaine was a senior in home economics the first year of her marriage—and she and Leon lived on a lean student budget. It was a time for drawing on all the resources of her food upbringing—how to make nutritious and filling meals with very little meat, how to waste almost nothing, how to depend on a garden and thus eat well without buying food at the grocery store!

That way of cooking and eating has been a developing theme for Elaine since then. In the early 70's she and Leon spent three

Elaine Good finds their farm and garden almost a complete resource for feeding her family. She's becoming expert at freeing herself and her cooking habits from overprocessed, overpackaged foods. Much of her concern stems from her and Leon's years in Africa under the Eastern Mennonite Board of Missions.

years in agriculture and community development in the country of Somalia, East Africa. That time became another primer for Elaine in starting-with-nearly-nothing-to-make-a-tasty-meal. Seldom burdened by the scarcity, it became her opportunity for creativity. And it gave the Goods a window on the world's food imbalance. That view moved their consciences and changed their menus.

Apple Pie

6 cups apples, peeled and sliced
3/4 cup sugar (vary according to the
apple's flavor)
1/4 cup flour
1 tsp. cinnamon
3 Tbsp. water
1 9" unbaked pie shell

Pour peeled and sliced apples into unbaked pie shell. Combine the sugar, flour, cinnamon, and water. Stir until smooth; then pour over the apples.

Cover with a top crust. Seal the edges. Bake at 375° for one hour.

Makes 1 9" pie

Make no mistake—the fun hasn't gone out of their eating! Elaine has simply done something about the discrepancy between America's eating habits and nutritional necessities. And she has allowed her cooking to be shaped by her rich food past *and* the world's food needs. For the Goods, with their four children, are back on the Good homestead in Lancaster County, operating the family dairy farm. The bounty is everywhere. They use it carefully.

"We've always had rhubarb," Elaine remembers. "It was a spring and summer dish that we ate either as a dessert or salad, depending on which the meal needed.

"But mainly my family asks for rhubarb crunch. Of all the dishes, that's my favorite. And it doesn't take nearly as much time as a pie. Less work and more servings! It's been our specialty for birthday parties.

Rhubarb Crunch

Crumbs

1 cup flour, sifted
1/2 cup brown sugar, firmly packed

7/7/92 Fair
Ruthie + Ron
liked it —
him + kids
for supper —
cool today 60°

1 tsp. cinnamon
3/4 cup oatmeal flakes
1/2 cup butter, melted
4 cups rhubarb, diced

Glaze

1/2 cup sugar
1 Tbsp. cornstarch
1 tsp. vanilla
1 cup water

Mix the crumbs until crumbly. Press half of them into a greased 9" x 9" baking pan. Cover with diced rhubarb.

Combine the glaze ingredients and cook until it thickens and clears. Pour it over the rhubarb. Top with the remaining crumbs; then bake at 350° for one hour.

Serve warm plain or with milk or ice cream.

Makes 8 servings.

"Ever since we've been married and have lived near a farm, we've used fresh raw milk. Along the way we decided to use it skimmed and save the cream for ice cream.

"We got our ice cream freezer about eight years ago. I didn't grow up with homemade ice cream. We used to have it on Saturday nights but it was always purchased.

"Frequently, now, we make our own, often on evenings other than the weekend because Saturday nights are so busy. And Leon always says he likes a little left over!

"We tend to prefer fruit ice creams but you can do anything with this recipe—add chocolate syrup or nuts—or fruit."

Ice Cream

3 eggs, beaten
2 cups granulated sugar
dash of salt
3 cups cream
2 tsp. vanilla
1 quart chopped fruit

Mix all the ingredients together well. Pour into freezer container, adding additional fruit or cream if necessary to make container 2/3 full.

Makes 4 quarts

14 Corn Pie Goes with Quilting

Ada Martin lives in one of those meandering farmsteads with a long front porch, a couple of front doors, and little additions here and there around the sides and back. Ada's husband, Jonathan, was born in the house. So was Jonathan's mother, Anna. In fact, Anna and her husband Abram still live on the homeplace. The older couple lives in the small end; Ada, Jonathan, and their nine children share the large part.

The three generations see each other constantly. The farming operation brings them together. What's more, both women like to quilt. In fact, they do such exquisite work that their quiltmaking has grown into a little business, some side income for each family.

Ada Hoover Martin learned to quilt at home before she was married. Years later her mother-in-law asked her to help piece some quilts she was making to sell. And now they each take quilt orders from shops. "Sometimes I piece, sometimes I quilt," Ada smiles. "It just depends on what I feel like that day."

The oldest of sixteen children, Ada learned early how to manage outdoor chores, household demands, and younger brothers and sisters. "I never knew anything but small children," she explains.

Two meals stand out from her growing-up years. "Saturdays we used to have mashed potatoes, pork, and sauerkraut. We stripped a lot of tobacco and that was our Saturday lunch."

And she still gets hungry for beef liver. "It was the first thing we made at home after we butchered! We would slice it, then roll it in flour and fry it in butter. We liked to cook it kinda quick so it

Everybody helps in a big family. That keeps gardening and farming from being over-whelming burdens. Ada and Jonathan Martin's daughters are seeding cherries, and they're becoming old hands at most other food preservation and preparation duties. They're having a good time and learning skills—both are useful in their Old Order Mennonite Community.

wouldn't get tough. Then we made a gravy from what was left in the pan for our mashed potatoes or noodles." Another good substantial meal. But one received with less enthusiasm by the Martin family than by the Hoovers!

Now some of the old Martin specialties have become regulars in Ada's kitchen. "Corn pie is something we all enjoy," she explains. And she learned how to make it by one of the most reliable methods possible—by watching her mother-in-law and then experimenting on her own. "We don't really have a recipe," she smiles. But Ada's caught the right touch, apparently. "Whenever one of us asks my husband what he wants for supper he'll ask for corn pie! We didn't make that at my home, but he ate a lot of it." And he still does!

Corn Pie

pastry for a two-crust pie
1 qt. corn
salt and pepper to taste
2 Tbsp. butter
milk

Line a casserole or deep pie pan with pastry. Pour in the corn; then season with salt and pepper. Dot with butter. Add milk just to moisten, but not so you can see it!

Cover with the top pastry, pinching the edges together to seal. Bake at 400° for 30-40 minutes or until the crust is browned and the corn is bubbly.

Makes 8 servings

Jonathan has struggled with weakening kidneys for several years. While he waits for a kidney transplant he needs to be on dialysis. It's a process that can be handled at home. So although his illness has been disruptive, the nearness of his parents and his and Ada's growing children has meant that the farm work can go on. When Jonathan feels well enough he can help. At the least he's nearby when counsel is needed.

Ada remembers that the nurse who came to put Jonathan on dialysis enjoyed her meals. In fact, she requested a little private tutoring. "She came one morning at seven o'clock to have me teach her how to bake bread!" Ada recalls. Breadbaking is a several hour affair and Ada wondered how she would keep this woman

66

occupied while they waited for the bread to rise. "My daughter suggested we make sticky buns, too, so then I worked the one dough while the nurse worked the other." It was a happy solution for everybody, since Ada confesses about the sticky buns, "I should make them oftener than I do, but they take a lot of time." To top off the day, Ada served corn pie to her family and the nurse for dinner. "She really liked that, too," Ada laughs modestly.

Ada grew up along the Conestoga Creek. In the Old Order Mennonite world where work is valued and accepted as natural and necessary, Sunday is the one day appropriate for rest and some recreation. After church, and after the dairying chores are done, of course. Ada remembers that on Sunday evenings when she was a teenager, the young people from the church would often picnic along their creek. Someone usually brought homemade O.Henry bars. "And when we finished eating, maybe we'd go for a ride in a boat," Ada explains.

O Henry Bars

1/2 cup butter
1/2 cup brown sugar
1/2 cup milk
1 cup graham crackers, crushed
1/2 cup nuts, chopped
1 cup coconut
whole graham crackers

Boil butter, brown sugar, and milk together for 1 minute. While the mixture is still hot add crushed graham crackers, chopped nuts, and coconut. Blend well.

Line the bottom of 9"x13" baking pan with whole graham crackers. Pour the filling over them. Then cover with another layer of whole graham crackers. Press down. When cool, spread with icing; then cut into serving pieces.

Icing

1 cup brown sugar
2 Tbsp. butter
3 Tbsp. milk
dash of vanilla
confectioners sugar

Mix together the brown sugar, butter, milk and vanilla. Bring to a boiling point, but do not allow to boil. Remove from heat and let cool a bit. Then stir in confectioners sugar until it reaches spreading consistency.

15 Managing a Surprise—and Sunday Lunch

When Edith Hess and David Thomas married, they brought together two clans rich in food know-how. The Thomases were beef and pork butchers; the Hesses took butter, cheese, eggs and chickens to Lancaster's weekly Southern Market.

That experience and knowledge has been paying off ever since. Edith and David became the parents of ten children, among them two sets of twins. Furthermore, David was ordained a minister and then a bishop. And for nineteen years he served as the moderator of Lancaster Mennonite Conference, a body of some 16,000 Mennonites. His leadership in the church brought scores of guests to the Thomas table. Yet in spite of all that, Edith still likes to cook—quickie meals for herself and David, or feasts for the tribe.

From the beginning, Edith found that food was a way to express affection. "Oh, coconut cake! We had a good time with that," she smiles. "It was always Mama's favorite cake, so on her birthday we children would find a way to get her out of the house. Papa would be out husking corn so we'd tell him he would have to take Mama out with him and keep her out a while because we had some work to do. First we had to crack the coconut shell and then grate the coconut meat.

"We baked a yellow cake and used white icing. Then we'd mix the coconut with granulated sugar and sprinkle it over the top of the cake. And Mama always acted surprised!

"A whole coconut made about 2½ cups of grated coconut so there would be a good bit left over from the cake. Mama would

Edith Thomas still likes a big garden, even though it's just she and David at home now. Who knows when one of their ten children (and family) may drop in? Or when she may need to cook for visiting church speakers? David's leadership among Lancaster Conference Mennonites has brought many guests to her table.

make tapioca, then spread real whipped cream over top and sprinkle it with coconut. That was good eating!

"We still make coconut cake, usually at Christmas. We tint the sugar pink and green, then mix it with the coconut."

Coconut Cake

2¼ cups flour
1 tsp. salt
3 tsp. baking powder
1½ cups sugar
1/2 cup margarine;
2/3 cup milk
1 tsp. vanilla
1/3 cup milk
2 eggs, unbeaten

Sift the dry ingredients. Add the margarine, 2/3 cup milk and vanilla. Beat 2 minutes; then add the remaining 1/3 cup milk and eggs. Beat 2 minutes more. Pour into greased layer pans. Bake at 350° for 30-35 minutes.

Frosting

3 cups 10x sugar
2 Tbsp. shortening
1 tsp. vanilla
2-3 Tbsp. milk
1 whole grated coconut (about 2½ cups)
1/2 cup granulated sugar

Put 10x sugar, shortening, vanilla, and milk in mixing bowl and beat until it is the right consistency to spread (more milk may be needed).

Frost cake. Combine the grated coconut and granulated sugar and sprinkle over the cake.

"When someone was sick at our house, the doctor would come and tell us to eat potato soup. He called me the 'Potato Soup Girl' because I always loved potatoes! I can eat them without butter . . . I just like the taste of potatoes!

"We always had potato soup Saturday noon when my parents were away at market. But I didn't make it so often for my own family because David didn't like it. So I'd make it when he was away, or I'd make tomato soup for him and potato soup for the rest of us. I always made it for the children when they were sick.

"I still get hungry for potatoes anytime—even at bedtime!"

Potato Soup

3-4 potatoes, peeled and diced
1/4 cup celery, chopped
1½ cup water
2 Tbsp. butter or margarine
1 quart milk
1 Tbsp. parsley
salt and pepper to taste
2 hardboiled eggs, diced

Cook the potatoes and celery in the water and butter until tender. Then add the milk, seasonings, and egg and heat thoroughly.

Makes 6 servings

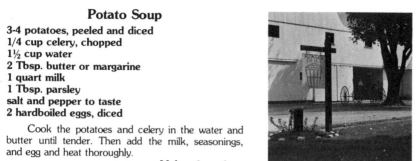

What do you feed ten hungry children on Sunday when you've all spent the morning in church and come home at lunchtime with stomachs roaring? "Roll meat and stewed crackers," remembers Edith. "It was quick! It didn't take as long as potatoes or noodles and the children liked it. Then we'd usually make peas or lima beans to go with it. We still eat stewed crackers. But not roll meat very often!"

Skyrocketing beef prices would put roll meat—a good beef brisket roll—nearly out of reach today. But it was feasible for a minister's large family because the Thomases were butchers. "I would cook the meat on Saturday, roasting it very slowly. I'd add just a little water and some salt and pepper. When it was tender I'd let it sit in the broth until it would congeal and sort of reabsorb the moisture. To eat it, we'd slice the meat into ¼-inch slices. It was a favorite meal for the children!"

Stewed Crackers

1/4-1/2 lb. (about 50 or 60) buttermilk, saltine,
  or round soup crackers
2½ cups milk
2 Tbsp. butter or margarine
3/4 cup milk

Butter the bottom and sides of a 1½ quart casserole. Lay dry crackers in the casserole. Heat the 2½ cups milk to scalding. Pour over crackers. Cover casserole and let stand at least 5 minutes, checking once to make sure the crackers are in the milk.

Just before serving, heat the butter until browned. Add 3/4 cup milk and warm it. Then pour browned butter and milk over the crackers.

Makes 4-5 servings

71

16 Still Baking Shoofly Pie and Roast

It can be hard to find Mary Zook at home these days. It seems she's either off quilting or entertaining her grandchildren, cleaning someone's house, or showing visiting friends the prime spots in the County. But although she's less housebound than when her four children were home, she can whip up a table full of food with little effort. She had lots of practice as a girl.

"I was the fifth oldest of sixteen children," Mary explains. "The second girl. When I was fourteen my older sister got married so I had to take over the cooking. It took three pies for each meal. So when I baked, I'd make eight shoofly pies, eight pumpkin, and eight crumb pies."

Mary's family was Old Order Amish. That meant their kitchen operated without electricity. And Mary remembers when they had no refrigerator, not even a gas powered one. But with such a large family there were few leftovers. And the farm and garden kept them freshly supplied with almost everything else they needed.

Mary still thinks in big quantities when she cooks. Her shoofly recipe produces "5 big pies or 6 little ones." But they freeze well, and, as she points out, "We entertain lots of company and I like to keep some on hand to eat with ice cream."

If the old dishes and their huge batches work for Mary, so do quickie meals that came from her home. She and her folk-artist husband savor one such standby. "I make cold milk soup for Aaron

Mary Zook got her cooking experience making meals for her parents and fifteen brothers and sisters. Everything was fresh (they had no refrigerator) and made from scratch. Mary and Aaron belong to the Beachy Amish church and entertain friends from there and from around the world. With every meal she puts her kitchen upbringing to use!

now if I'm short on time. You take a piece of bread—homemade is best—and crumble it up. Then you put milk and sugar on it, and finally cold sliced fruit or nuts over top. We like fresh strawberries or blueberries or peaches. I enjoy it most when the soup's really cold."

The dish belongs to Mary's world—wonderfully refreshing, the ingredients are all at hand, and it's economical, time-wise and cost-wise.

Shoo Fly Pie

Bottom Part

1 cup brown sugar
1 egg
1 cup molasses
1/2 tsp. soda
1/3 cup boiling water
2/3 cup cold water

Crumbs

2 cups flour
2/3 cup brown sugar
1/3 tsp. baking powder
1/2 cup shortening or lard

Begin with the Bottom Part by stirring the egg into 1 cup of brown sugar. Add the molasses. Dissolve the baking soda in the boiling water. Add the cold water; then combine with the sugar and egg mixture. Pour into an unbaked 9" pie shell.

Cut the flour, brown sugar, baking powder, and shortening together until crumbly. Sprinkle on top of the Bottom Part.

Bake at 350° for 10 minutes. Reduce heat to 325° and bake 50 minutes longer, or until done.

Makes 1 9" pie

Mary's butterscotch cookies were her brother Jake's specialty. "Jake liked to bake. We used to get up at 5 o'clock. The milking would be done about 6:00 so we'd have to have breakfast ready then. Before 7:30 we ate and washed dishes, and then ran all the way to school to be there by 8:00. Jake would mix up the cookies after he was done in the barn. Then we'd stand around with our lunch boxes waiting for them to come out of the oven. He wouldn't get them all baked before we'd have to leave!"

74

Butterscotch Cookies

2 cups brown sugar
3 eggs
1 cup shortening or lard
4 cups flour
1 tsp. baking soda
1 tsp. cream of tartar
1 cup nuts

Mix all ingredients but the nuts thoroughly in a mixer. Stir the nuts in by hand.

Roll the dough into ropes about 2 inches thick. Cut in thin slices. Cross-press with a fork to make a design.

Bake at 350° for 8-12 minutes.

Makes 7-8 dozen

"Roast" is the main dish served at Old Order Amish weddings in Lancaster County. Usually it's made with chicken. But at Mary Beiler and Aaron Zook's wedding, the meat was duck. "My Dad raised Muscovy ducks," Mary explains. "And people fussed about that because duck isn't dry.

"We often made roast for thrashers. We'd have as many as twenty-two at a time, and those men would eat. They always said, 'We like to go to Abe Beiler's house to eat!' " Mary still makes roast. It, too, freezes well.

Chicken Roast

1½ loaf homemade bread
1 lb. butter or margarine
1½ tsp. salt
1/2 tsp. pepper
1 tsp. celery seed
3/4 cup celery, chopped (optional)
meat from a whole chicken, stewed and removed from bones

Crumble the bread by hand into a large mixing bowl. Melt the butter; then pour it over the bread crumbs. Add the seasonings and chopped celery. Then mix with the deboned chicken chunks.

Turn into a large roast pan and bake covered at 350° for a half hour to an hour, until heated through. Dampen with water around the edge if it begins to dry out. Stir often to prevent sticking.

Note: You may make a rich gravy to serve over the roast by thickening the chicken broth with flour.

17 Memories of Mush and Cracker Pudding

Living under the same roof as Grandpa and Grandma is more than quaint history for Becky and John Jacob Oberholtzer. Things have gone something like this—John Jacob brought his bride, Becky Stoner, to the homeplace in 1946 so they could run the farm. Being newlyweds, they set up housekeeping in a few rooms that had been carved out of the less central part of the farm house. Then when their children began arriving, they eventually spread into the whole house. The older couple moved to be neighbors to one of their daughters and her family.

Now Becky and John Jacob's children are on their own, and Grandpa and Grandma Oberholtzer are growing old and ailing. So once again the homestead has been turned back into a two-family house. This time the elderly Oberholtzers are in the young people's end, just off the big kitchen. Where Becky first learned how to cook on a woodstove, she now prepares meals for her mother-in-law who gave her those early lessons.

A few dishes have remained family favorites through the whole cycle of events. "My mother-in-law showed me how to make corn-meal mush in an iron kettle on top of our cookstove. And I still make it for them and for us," Becky explains.

Mush is hearty, simple to make, and economical. It's a stick-to-the-ribs food that's especially satisfying in the winter-time. And it can be eaten in a variety of forms. "Right after you cook it you can eat it as a hot cereal with milk. I like it that way for lunch with honey and butter," says Becky. "I used to always make a batch that was

Becky Oberholtzer knows how to add a special touch to old-fashioned food. She adjusts the recipe just a trifle to make it more attractive or more healthful, and then serves the result in an exquisite old dish—cracker pudding, for instance. Becky stands on market, cares for her parents-in-law, and belongs to a neighboring Lancaster Conference Mennonite church.

enough mush for ten days. What was left after our cereal meal I would put in long loaf pans until it 'set up.' Then I sliced it about one-half inch thick and fried it."

Becky learned critical timing. "In the wintertime when the children were small I sliced the mush, put it in the pan, went out to the barn for about forty-five minutes to carry milk, then came in and turned it to have it ready to eat when John Jacob came in. We have always liked it crisp."

Then what? "You can eat it with molasses or pork pudding. Just heat the pudding and pour it over the mush like gravy. Then you ought to have pickled red beets with it yet, to kind of cut the grease." This is a diet clearly meant for the physically active!

Corn Meal Mush

1 quart cold water
1 quart boiling water
2 cups roasted yellow corn meal
1 tsp. salt

Put cold water in a bowl. Combine the corn meal and salt and stir into the cold water.

Bring the other quart of water to a boil. Slowly add the cornmeal and cold water mixture to it, stirring constantly to prevent lumps. When smooth, cover and cook slowly from 1-3 hours, just so the mush glops slowly.

Becky has other favorite dishes with a cornmeal base. "Cornmeal pancakes came from my home. They get thicker and crispier around the edges than regular ones. They used to be our summer breakfast. Now we eat them for lunch or supper, sometimes with dried beef gravy. Our oldest son who's been away from home for ten years still asks for them."

Corn Meal Pancakes

1/2 cup flour
1½ cups roasted yellow corn meal
2 tsp. baking powder
1 Tbsp. sugar
1 tsp. salt
1½ cups milk
1 Tbsp. liquid shortening

Combine all ingredients. Mix well. Fry on greased griddle or skillet until browned.

Makes about 20 cakes

"Cracker pudding is a dish that comes from my Grandma Stoner. She served it to company. Her daughter-in-law, my mother, made it once in a while. Now the menfolk expect me to serve it often! It is John Jacob's favorite dessert."

Becky likes to pass cookies around the table with her pudding. And she has come up with her own adaptation of the old recipe. "My Grandma made it with beaten egg whites spread on top of the finished pudding, which she then browned like a meringue. My recipe is a hybrid. I fold the beaten whites into the pudding, then it's lighter and less coarse. You can also serve it in a prettier dish if you don't have to bake it."

Cracker Pudding

6 cups milk
3 eggs, separated
3/4 cup sugar
3 cups fine saltine cracker crumbs
1¼ cups coconut
1 tsp. vanilla

Scald the milk. Beat egg yolks; then add sugar and blend. Add gradually to the milk, stirring constantly. Cook for one minute; then add the cracker crumbs and coconut. Stir until the mixture thickens and the crumbs soften.

Beat the egg whites until stiff. Then fold them and the vanilla into the pudding while it is still hot. Chill and serve.

Makes 6-8 servings

Becky ranks as a topnotch hostess. She enjoys dusting off the old china, shining up the good family glassware, and putting together an old-fashioned menu that is also mindful of today's more sedentary lifestyle. "I like to have guests," Becky smiles. "And I like to figure out meals that go together, that are balanced, and that look attractive." It's a combination she has mastered.

18 Pot Pie or Cookies for Company

Sadie Beiler cooks on the run. That doesn't mean, however, that she opens tin cans or depends on boxed mixes. It's just that she has never had the time to cook for recreation. She cooks simply, because people at her house get hungry.

Neither the farming operation nor the printing business can be ignored at the Beiler homestead. And over the years, Joseph and Sadie, along with their eight daughters and one son, have been busy in both of those enterprises. "Our eating is according to our work," Sadie chuckles as she turns away from her sewing machine. "If we have a lot of printing, we just sort of skimp. At this house it's meals at all hours whenever it's convenient!"

Joseph was born in the house where he and Sadie raised their family and still live. For most of their married life they ran the farm. Then in the late sixties, Joseph who is a minister in the Old Order Amish church, began a magazine called *The Diary*. He and other church leaders sensed a need to provide reading matter—and "glue"—to give their people a greater sense of belonging to each other. Not only was Joseph the editor; he also became the printer. Along the way, he also began publishing books.

Now there's one way a full-time farmer can become a full-time printer/publisher—with lots of help from his wife and children! And because Christian is the Beilers' only son, Sadie and the girls spent a lot of time outdoors. "The work outside has always taken us away from the kitchen," Sadie explains. "When our children were small one woman told me that I'd be busier than if I had had three boys.

Joseph and Sadie Beiler's farm lacks almost nothing. Except chickens! A busy operation, the farm, family, and printing business have all required Sadie's attention. What's more, she and Joseph regularly entertain guests from around the world.

With all girls, I'd be needed inside and out." And it's turned out to be true. But Sadie hasn't minded.

"I was the youngest daughter in a family of twelve. I was to 'go and get it' and my mother would make it! Even when I went to help my older married brothers and sisters, I'd often do the cleaning or help with the baby, and they'd cook. I still like to push the cooking off on our girls!"

But somehow Sadie learned the essentials from her mother whose hectic schedule foreshadowed her own. "Chicken pot pie was a good dish for us when I was a girl at home. Mom liked to make it whenever we had men for silo filling or haymaking. We always had chickens, so she'd kill a few in the morning and we'd have them for lunch. Whenever we had unexpected company we could go kill a chicken! Now when we're driving and pass some chickens running around, I get so hungry I think we ought to have some on our farm.

"Chicken pot pie is a meat-saving dish. Now, it's not a quick thing. Mom always had onions and potatoes on hand to put in. And she'd make the pot pie noodles right then. She didn't keep a supply of them on hand. When I make pot pie I put in some carrots, too, for flavor and color. It's a good meal to make when our children come to visit."

Chicken Pot Pie

1 3½-4 lb. chicken
4 medium-sized potatoes, peeled and cut
    into chunks
1 onion, diced
salt and pepper to taste
pot pie squares

Cook the chicken in two quarts water until it is partly tender. Then add the onion and potatoes and cook until they and the chicken are completely tender. Remove meat from bones and set aside.

Bring broth to a boil. Drop pot pie squares into boiling broth and cook 20 minutes or until tender. Return chicken to the broth and serve steaming hot.

Pot Pie Dough

2 eggs
2 cups flour
2-3 Tbsp. milk or cream

Break the eggs into the flour. Work together, adding the milk or cream to make a soft dough. Roll out the dough as thin as possible and cut into 1"x2" rectangles with a knife or pastry wheel. Drop into boiling broth.

Makes 8 servings

The Amish are used to lots of unannounced, drop-in company. Plentiful food—either from the garden or canning shelves—keeps the cook from panicking.

Sadie has discovered that cookie-baking is a good thing to do with guests. "I mix a big batch of sugar cookies and only bake half of them at a time. The other half I keep in the refrigerator for up to two to three weeks. What I like is if someone comes, then you have something to do. And the cookies are much better, too, when they're fresh!"

Sugar Cookies

4½ cups brown sugar
2 cups lard, melted
2 cups sour cream
8 eggs
3 tsp. soda
3 tsp. cream of tartar
9 cups flour
1 Tbsp. vanilla
pinch of salt

Cream the sugar and lard. Add the sour cream and eggs and beat well. Stir in the remaining ingredients and mix well.

Drop by teaspoons onto greased cookie sheets. Bake at 325° 8-10 minutes.

In the last year, the typesetting equipment and word processor (all run by a generator in this home without electricity), the paper supply and book inventory have outgrown the Beilers' house. So Joseph and his son, Christian, built a piece on the shed to accommodate the printing business.

Now that the machinery is gone, Joseph and Sadie are moving into the small end of the house. Christian and his bride are settling into the big part of the house. Christian is taking over the farm, but Joseph and Sadie are far from retiring!

19 A Farm Can Feed a Family—and More

Nora Hoover still enjoys cooking, despite the fact that at age fourteen she assumed responsibility for feeding her eight brothers and sisters, and then had a family of ten of her own to keep filled. "It seems I get at my cooking before my cleaning," she smiles.

In large families the older children shoulder sizable duties in the house, out-of-doors, and with their younger brothers and sisters. Early on, girls and boys become reliable cooks, milkers, and baby entertainers.

Hard as it was when Nora's mother got tuberculosis, Nora managed. "I was the oldest girl," she explains. "There were nine of us. The baby was eight months old then and I had just turned fourteen. My mother was in the sanitarium in Lancaster for a year and a half."

Once a week she baked a cake—angel food! "That was one cake I could make. My brother just talked about it recently! That was one cake they always got!" Made-from-scratch angel food cakes turn out best if you work without an electric mixer, advises Nora. "If you beat the eggs too fast the foam goes down. I always used a wire whisk at home." Angel food is a cake requiring lots of care and lots of eggs. Care is a hallmark of any good cook. Eggs are abundant on most farms. So although angel food cakes are special, in farm kitchens they're not considered extravagant.

Nora, her husband, Amos, and their six children who are still at home, live on a farm near Denver. They raise hogs, and collect books and historical data related to the various Mennonite and

84

Nora Hoover has spent hours - and years - in the kitchen. But she still enjoys it. Countless family meals, days of canning and freezing, and two weddings have taken place on this Old Order Mennonite family's farm.

Amish groups. Their Muddy Creek Historical Library is an unusually complete and well-organized collection of many rare materials.

Angel Food Cake

1½ cups cake flour
2¼ cups granulated sugar
2¼ cups egg whites (18 eggs)
3 Tbsp. water
1/4 tsp. salt
1½ tsp. cream of tartar
1½ tsp. vanilla

Sift the flour. Add 3/4 cup sugar and sift with flour three times. Set aside.

Beat the egg whites with a rotary beater (not an electric mixer) until foamy. Add salt and cream of tartar. Continue beating until the whites hold peaks. Slowly add the rest of the sugar to the beaten egg whites, folding it in gently. Add the vanilla.

Sift the flour and sugar mixture, a tablespoon at a time, over the beaten egg whites. Fold in lightly.

Pour well blended mixture into a 12-14 inch ungreased tube pan. Bake at 350° for one hour. When finished, turn the cake upside down to cool. Frost with a butter icing if desired.

Amos learned to value old things from early association with his mother's parents. "I went to live with my Burkholder grandparents when I was three," he explains, "And I really got an edge on old stories."

From his grandfather he also learned to enjoy another delicacy—mushroom soup. For a year after his grandmother died, the two of them had no cook. "Grandfather's married daughters would bring us food during the week, but for Sunday dinners we were on our own. Then we would make that delicious soup. I believe," smiles Amos, "I'm the only Old Order Mennonite who knows how to make and get hungry for mushroom soup!"

Amos' enthusiasm for mushrooms has spread to his own family. Nora concocted a mushroom gravy that she says "is a treat when we have it." She begins with fresh mushrooms, cuts them in pieces, steams them gently in butter, then adds milk which she thickens a bit. "We eat it on toast bread like a gravy." It's a delicious departure from custom for this family who values tradition highly!

Weddings, among the Old Order Mennonites, almost always take place at the home of the bride. And they're not small, private affairs. With large families and a close church fellowship, a couple is likely to invite between 200 and 300 guests. The reception following the ceremony is usually a complete meal, served in the home, and prepared by the bride's immediate family. Naturally, the mother of the bride carries most of that responsibility.

"Two of our daughters have had weddings at our house," says Nora. "For Rosemarie's there were about 250 people. We probably had more kinds of food than we needed, but she wanted some things and I wanted some things!"

What was the menu? "We had pork roll made from our own hogs. We sliced it thick and heated it in the oven. It doesn't make a lot of drippings so the ham broth for gravy came from the nearby meat stand. Then we had buns and noodles—the noodles we made ourselves!—peas and carrots, cole slaw, and a vegetable platter with celery and carrot sticks, pickles and olives, raw mushrooms and cauliflower. We set bowls of cheese chunks and pretzel thins on the table and dishes of party mix with nuts.

"For dessert we had fruit salad with jello mixed in, a strawberry danish dessert, and then two kinds of sheet cake—chocolate and vanilla—with three kinds of ice cream, each a different color. We scooped out the balls of ice cream ahead of time and piled them in dishes which we passed. Then Rosemarie made mints. Each person got a little three-ounce cup full of them."

A rich meal for a blessed occasion. In the food is a message of love for the bride, groom, and guests alike, and a reminder that marriage is awesome and sacred.

Mints

4 Tbsp. butter (or 3 oz. softened cream cheese)
3 Tbsp. sweetened condensed milk
1 lb. 10X sugar
½ tsp. mint flavoring
food coloring
granulated sugar

Mash butter or cream cheese with milk. Gradually add sugar until the mixture is like stiff pie dough.

Work in the flavoring and the food coloring until the mixture reaches the desired shade.

Roll into small balls, then roll in granulated sugar. Press into candy molds, and then unmold immediately. (The mints freeze well.)

Makes 90 mints

20 Growing Up on Corn Pone and Stewed Apples

As a child, I had a double blessing, food-wise. If, for some rare reason, Ma couldn't make supper, Daddy did. He enjoyed it and so did the rest of us.

Richard Pellman's standards are high—good flavor without compromising health! He regularly packed our lunches, trying to steer us toward "quality" sandwich meat. And when he made breakfast, we could count on a hot, grainy cereal, rich in memory and nutrition for him, but less loved by the rest of us!

Daddy is an adept cook. He got his tutorship as the second child in a family of eight and later in a moonlighting job as a butcher. His career has been as sales manager of a dairy; there his special beat has been quality control. And with equal seriousness and pleasure he helps select the firm's ice cream flavors.

The men have been cooks in the Pellman family for several generations. "My Grandpa Pellman physically got in there and helped," Daddy recalls. "Whenever his family came home there was always a big gang. And I remember he wore a white apron. Then my Dad got into it too, not so much the actual preparation as the management. And I liked to be busy; I didn't like seeing things that weren't done. So we all just chipped in to keep things afloat."

Sometimes he was primarily the dish washer. But he still watched what was going on. "I learned combinations then—what foods went together—like a ham hock with green beans. Or if we had tomato sauce, we usually had mashed potatoes. Then, very likely, the meat was pork or beef. For me it was always a toss-up between

Richard Pellman keeps turning up in the kitchen because he likes it there! As much as the completion of a recipe, he enjoys the production of it—the feel of ripe tomatoes, full berries, cornmeal sifting through his fingers.

This is my Dad—his career has been in food production; his commitment has been to his family and local Mennonite church.

89

eating gravy or tomato sauce on the mashed potatoes!"

There were certain seasonal reasons for particular food combinations. And Grandpa Pellman had learned how to balance taste and make a complete meal nutritionally. Daddy remembers that they served tomato sauce and warm slaw as vegetables. "They were old recipes in the family. And a lot of the meal combinations were also passed along. They, too, were tried! During the fall and winter when we butchered at home, we always had cabbage. So we'd have warm slaw with beef liver."

Warm Slaw

2 Tbsp. butter
1 quart shredded cabbage
1 tsp. salt
1½ cups water
5 Tbsp. sugar
1 egg, beaten
1 Tbsp. flour
1/2 cup milk
2 Tbsp. vinegar

Melt butter in saucepan and add cabbage. Stir thoroughly; then add salt and water. Cover and cook 10 minutes.

In a bowl mix sugar, egg, flour, and milk. Add to the cabbage. Cook another minute. Add the vinegar and serve.

Makes 4 servings

Daddy learned to love food in its prime. "When you help pick peas and beans and gather potatoes, you feel the freshness of the vegetables. You develop a feel for the maturity, the ripeness. Our tomato sauce had such a great tomato flavor because we never used half-green tomatoes. They were ripe!"

Sometimes Grandpa loaded up his gang and headed into the neighboring mountains to forage for berries or wild cherries. Once again the children handled plump and ready fruit.

Daddy remembers that sometimes they made their own corn meal. "Dad would bring in some young field corn and roast it in the oven on the cob. Then we'd take it to the mill and have it stone ground." Corn meal was a handy commodity that could be turned into breakfast, dinner, or supper food. "For breakfasts," Daddy recalls, "we ate mush made from our own corn meal and pudding

from our own pork. We had cornflakes only if company came!"
Then there was corn pone. The freshly baked bread was a meal.

Corn Pone

1 cup sugar
1/2 cup butter or shortening
2 eggs
1½ cups cornmeal
1½ cups flour
3 tsp. baking powder
1/2 tsp. salt
1½ cups milk

Cream sugar and shortening. Add eggs and beat well. Combine cornmeal, flour, baking powder, and salt. Add alternately with milk.

Pour into a greased and floured 9" x 13" cake pan or two round layer cake pans. Bake at 350° for 45 minutes.

Fills one 9" x 13" pan

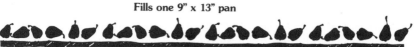

Daddy introduced another treat to our family—stewed apples with raisins. His father had brought the dish to his brood. Daddy remembers, "My Dad loved stewed apples, especially with mush. They were kind of a dessert, even for breakfast. Or if we were hungry before we went to bed and there were stewed apples around, they made a great finish!"

Stewed apples with raisins have now been taste tested by the fourth generation. Our daughters put away four helpings at a Saturday lunch not long ago. Daddy wasn't a bit surprised. Nor was I. He had simply passed on his gift to our family's food tradition—fruit presented in its full ripeness with no distraction from its natural flavor.

Stewed Apples

2 quarts apples
1/3-1/2 cup sugar
1½-2 cups raisins

Core and quarter the apples. Peel them if you like. Add sugar according to taste and the sweetness of the apples and raisins.

Pour into a saucepan and add an inch or two of water. Add raisins to taste.

Cook *slowly*, stirring up frequently, only until the "rawness is broken down. Then stop!"

A Word about Our People . . .

The Mennonites, Amish, and Brethren in Christ are much like an extended family. With many branches, each with its own particularities, the groups are still more alike than different.

In this cookbook are stories of cooks who are members of some of these more predominant groups found in Lancaster County, Pennsylvania. Most of these churches also have members throughout much of North America.

The Mennonites, Amish, Brethren in Christ and River Brethren all have common faith rooting. Their beginning can be traced to the time of the Protestant Reformation in sixteenth-century Europe. In 1525 a group of believers parted company with the established state church for a variety of reasons. Among them was the conviction that one must voluntarily become a follower of Christ, and that that deliberate decision will be reflected in all of one's life. Therefore, baptism must symbolize that choice. The movement was nicknamed "Anabaptism," meaning re-baptism, since the believers wanted to be baptized again as adults.

Eventually the group were called Mennonites after Menno Simons, one of their leaders who had formerly been a Roman Catholic priest. Over the years these people grew into a strong faith community, concerned with the nurture and discipline of each other.

Basic to their beliefs was a conviction that if one was a faithful follower of Christ's, one's behavior would clearly distinguish one from the larger world. These people saw themselves as separated unto God because of their values of love, forgiveness and peace. Because they were misunderstood and because they appeared to be a threat to the established church and government, the people were often persecuted and many became refugees.

In 1693, a charismatic young Mennonite leader believed that the church was losing some of its purity and that it was beginning to compromise with the world. And so he and a group who agreed with him left the Mennonites and formed a separate fellowship. They were called Amish, after their leader, Jacob Amman. Today the Amish identify themselves as the most conservative group of Mennonites.

Both the Mennonites and Amish have split and realigned many

times throughout the years. In some cases, personality conflicts were the reasons. But most often the concerns were about the need for maintaining purity and faithfulness within the church. How that should be done and to what degree are the critical questions that have often resulted in division.

While the various Mennonite and Amish groups have few doctrinal differences, they differ most in specific practices. In general, the Amish tend to be more wary of interchange with the larger world. They are more distinctly separate in lifestyle. The Old Order Amish do not own or drive cars, they live without electricity, have prescribed dress patterns, operate their own schools, and speak Pennsylvania Dutch among themselves, a language which further defines their group. They are also cautious about doing missions.

In general, the Mennonites have been more open to give-and-take with the larger world, accepting technology and education, being less distinctively different in lifestyle, and being active in mission work. They have fostered group identity by working at making church central to social life and Christian faith the motivation for one's training or choice of job or how one uses money.

But none of these are static people. Nor are these generalizations categorically true. There are Amish groups who use technology and promote higher learning. And there are Mennonites who drive horses and buggies, follow nonconformity in their dress and prefer farm-related occupations.

For instance, the Amish Mennonite groups, sometimes called the Beachy Amish after their founder, have vigorous mission programs. And although their dress patterns reflect their Old Order Amish connections, they drive cars, use electricity, and many send their children to high school.

The Old Order Mennonite group, nicknamed Wenger Mennonites after their leader, drive horses and carriages, dress very distinctively and do not actively practice missions. Another Old Order Mennonite group, the Horning Mennonites, do drive cars, but with the chrome painted black in many cases, and have electricity in their homes.

Lancaster Conference Mennonites are the largest group of Mennonites in Lancaster County. In addition, their churches spread along the eastern United States seaboard. The churches in this

Conference vary a great deal in practice, but most would favor formal education and would actively support a large worldwide mission and relief program. Their dress patterns have undergone significant change in the last generation, so that in many congregations, nearly all distinction is gone. In addition, many of these people are no longer farming (for reasons of economics, education or personal preference) so they have moved into the trades and professions.

The Amish of Lancaster County, and the Mennonites, both the Old Order and most Lancaster Conference groups, trace their ancestry to Germany and Switzerland. But there is another large stream of Mennonites whose heritage reaches back to the Netherlands, Prussia, and Russia. Their route to the New World was a quite different one because of both persecution and economics. Consequently, their traditions vary also, because of the places they migrated to and from. In North America, they settled largely in the Canadian and United States Mid-West.

A few Anabaptist groups began in Lancaster County. The River Brethren emerged after a revival movement swept the area in the 1780's. In addition to new converts, members came to the new group from Mennonite, Baptist, and Lutheran churches. So the fellowship was flavored with Anabaptism and pietism.

Some time during the mid-1850's the Brethren divided over a variety of issues, among them, how to most properly live the faith-life. Those who chose the more traditional path, including distinctive dress and transportation, as well as caution toward the larger world, became known as Old Order River Brethren.

The other group was called the Brethren in Christ. They, too, emphasized disciplined, nonconformed living along with a zest for devotionalism, expressed with emotion. Those basic elements are strong today in this part of the church that also has strong mission activity.

The total North American population of all the groups in this faith family now surpasses 300,000. One-tenth of those people live in Lancaster County. While that gives Lancaster the largest combined numbers of Mennonites, Amish, Brethren in Christ and related groups, these people are still a minority. They make up less than one-tenth of the county's total population.

Index

The Author and Photographer

The author and the photographer with their parents, Betty and Richard Pellman.

Phyllis Pellman Good, a Lancaster County native, is editor of *Festival Quarterly,* a magazine exploring the art, faith, and culture of Mennonite peoples. Together, she and her husband, Merle, direct The People's Place and The Old Country Store in Intercourse, Pennsylvania and publish Good Books.

Phyllis is the author of *Paul and Alta,* coeditor of *Perils of Professionalism,* coauthor with Merle of *20 Most Asked Questions about the Amish and Mennonites,* and coeditor of twelve Pennsylvania Dutch Cookbooklets.

Phyllis received her BA and MA in English from New York University. For ten years she and Merle produced and directed original plays at the Festival Theater in Lancaster.

The Goods are the parents of two daughters and members of the Landisville Mennonite Church.

Kenneth R. Pellman has been Manager of The People's Place since 1980. He previously managed The Dutch Family Festival and acted in its Festival Theater.

A graduate of Eastern Mennonite College, Kenny taught drama in the College's English department for one year.

Kenny is married to Rachel Thomas. The Pellmans have one son and are members of Rossmere Mennonite Church.